Get Home Safe

When the SHTF

Build the Perfect Get Home Bag

Airek Windslayer

Disclaimer:

Care has been taken to offer precise and accurate information within this book. However the information described within is for informational purposes only and must be verified by professionals in each relevant field discussed. Always seek professional instruction before using any equipment, method, or idea presented within this book. Neither the author nor the publisher is responsible for any damage, injury, or death that can result from using the information contained herein.

Contents

Foreword

I go to the School of Hard Knocks. I don't know why people say they graduated from the School of Hard Knocks because anyone who's ever "attended" knows damn well you never graduate; it's an ongoing course that lasts a lifetime. I was taught at a young age to fix things when they broke, many things have dual uses (at least), and a knife is a tool and tools have to be used and kept in working order.

When I initially set out to write this book I mentioned it to a fellow prepper. I was asked "How are you going to write a book about prepping? You're not even a professional!" I was dumbfounded; I've been into prepping since I was 15 or 16 years old, except they called it a Survivalist back then. I realized how unprepared I was after 9/11 happened and that's when I started taking it seriously. Then I wondered, is there really any such thing as a *professional prepper*? I don't think there is; there are preppers that have more arrogance than me, there are preppers that have more disposable income than I do and can buy all those amazing and expensive toys that you must own if you want to live, and there are more, a whole lot more preppers that have a better line of bullshit than I do. But are they *Professional*? No, there's no such thing. But there are people that have lived through some crazy shit that are out their sharing their survival experience, men like Selco and Fernando "FerFAL" Aguirre. Selco is from the Balkan region of Eastern Europe who lived "...one whole year and survived in a city without electricity, fuel, running water, real food distribution, or distribution of any goods, or any kind of organized law or government." Selco shares his knowledge at shtfschool.com. And Fernando "FerFAL" Aguirre has lived through the Argentine socio-economic collapse of 2001, and shares his experiences in his book, *The Modern*

Survival Manual: Surviving the Economic Collapse. If there are any professional preppers in the world, these men are examples of two of them.

When the SHTF

There are many ways a SHTF scenario can happen, there are scenarios like natural disasters such as floods, hurricanes, and fires. Then there's civil unrest like we witnessed in the 1992 L.A. Riots, and the disgusting antics of Antifa that are happening now. These are localized disasters and do not affect the entire country or the world. The information contained in these pages will certainly help in any one these localized events, but this book was written for a catastrophe that will change the end of the world as we know it, or as it is referred to in the prepper community as TEOTWAWKI.

I feel that an attack on the power grid through terrorism or a High Altitude EMP Strike (HEMP, but will be referred to as an EMP in this book) against the United States is a real threat and probably the most likely event that will happen, next to an Economic Collapse. Even if an event like this does not occur, being prepared for such an event will make minor events more comfortable to deal with.

EMP Attack

A High Altitude EMP is caused by a nuclear explosion in the atmosphere. An explosion like this creates an intense field of energy in the atmosphere; this energy makes its way down and out, in a cone shape to the surface and is spread out over a large area. It will reach the ground within a second after the explosion and wreak havoc to any solid state electronic in the affected area. The greater the altitude of the EMP explosion the greater the surface area will be affected. An explosion at the height of 30 miles will cover a radius of almost 500 miles. 120 miles in the atmosphere will cover a 1000 mile radius, and at a height of 300 miles up a radius of almost 1500 miles will be affected. This immense burst of energy will completely destroy the power grid; transformers will explode and every relay station along the way will be fried along with every computer, generator, and mode of transportation. Some automobiles will be affected and some won't. Not enough tests have been done because of the large expense of testing vehicles, but of the cars that are not affected by the EMP, gasoline will be very scarce if not impossible to get because it takes electricity to operate the pumps.

If Terrorists plane a coordinated attack against the power grid they can easily knock out the power to the entire country. If this type of attack happens all your electronics will still be intact, however, transportation will still be crippled because there will be no electricity to operate fuel pumps. And it is very likely that the government will place restrictions on the gas that is available.

We all know that when the lights go out bad people like to do bad things. I've read a few things that say riots and looting will start within a month after a grid down situation. Whoever says this has never been in New York City during a six hour blackout! The riots and looting will happen almost immediately and escalate quickly by no later than the following day. In a report to Congress, The EMP Commission states that after an EMP event, 90% of the population will be dead within a year due to starvation, disease, and civil unrest. I don't agree with this estimate, I give it six months.

I put together a timeline of events that *I feel* will happen if the grid ever does go down. This timeline is by no means perfect and does not cover everything, but it gives a general idea of what we'll be dealing with.

Timeline After an EMP

Within 1 Second:
- No electricity.
- No transportation.
- No communications, no cell phones, internet, television, radio.
- No food delivery.
- Food production ceases.

Within 24 Hours:
- Riots in Cities and Suburbs.
- Civil Unrest.
- Drug Addicts going through withdrawals.
- Alcoholics going through withdrawals.
- Food stores empty.

Within 72 Hours:
- Looting and civil unrest worsens.
- People suffer and die from drinking contaminated water.
- People dead from excessive heat or by freezing to death.
- People relying on life support systems are dead.
- Feral Dogs.

Within 1 Week:
- Medications start running low.
- Deaths from disease.
- Riots and Civil unrest worsens, gangs form.
- People start eating domestic pets.

Within 1 Month:
- People dead from starvation.
- Medications run out.
- People on antidepressants and antipsychotic drugs go through withdrawals.
- More deaths from civil unrest.
- Looting becomes more organized and widespread.
- Cannibalism.
- Murder, Rape, and kidnapping are commonplace.

Within 6 Months:
- 70 to 90% of population dead from starvation, disease, and civil unrest.

I apologize for sugar coating this timeline.

Economic Collapse

An Economic Collapse might start with an Emergency Bank Holiday. A regular bank holiday is when the banks close for the day in recognition of a normal holiday like Christmas or Thanksgiving. That's normal and we know the banks will reopen the following day; the reason for an emergency holiday is an emergency closure to avert a Bank Run. A Bank Run is when people literally run to the bank to withdraw cash from their accounts because they're afraid they'll lose their money due to the bank becoming insolvent.

Banks operate on a Fractional-Reserve banking system which is exactly what it sounds like; they only keep a fractional amount of the money in reserve, this reserve is about 10% of the actual cash the books represent. In a financial crisis the banks fear that everyone will run to the bank to take out all their money. They can't give everyone back all their money because they don't have it. So they will take a holiday and close so nobody will be able to withdraw their money. ATM's will be shut down along with online banking; you will not be able get any of your money or pay any of your bills during an emergency bank holiday such as this. The Great Depression was the result of bank runs after the stock market crash in 1929.

This not only happened in the United States in the past but also in Germany to the Weimar Republic in the early 1920's, in Argentina in 1998 to 2002 where they experienced a Great Depression of their own. And also in Venezuela since 2012 and is still going on today at the time of this writing in 2017.

To get an idea of what goes on during an economic collapse read *The Modern Survival Manual: Surviving the Economic Collapse*, written by Fernando "Ferfal" Aguirre, a survivor of the Economic Collapse in Argentina.

Getting Home

The "Rule of Three" says you can only live; *3 minutes without air, 3 hours without shelter (in extreme conditions), 3 days without water, 3 weeks without food.* When you put together a Get Home Bag, or GHB, you have to consider Food, Water, Shelter, Fire, Navigation, and Security. Food, water, and shelter are the three basic needs of survival. Fire is used in each of these basic needs: to cook your food, to sterilize your water, and to keep you warm in your shelter. Anything that protects you from the elements is considered shelter and this also includes your clothing. Navigation will cover two more important subjects: the distance you have to travel and the type of terrain you have to travel over. Terrain includes conditions that will help you or hinder you in your progress, like weather, hostile animals, and natural or manmade obstacles. Security of course is the ability to make sure no-one or nothing tries to take your other survival needs away from you.

Your GHB should be assembled according to how far you have to travel and the conditions you'll be traveling in. After you put your GHB together it will live most of its life in the trunk of your car. Or if you use public transportation to get to work you might want to keep one at your workplace and another in your car so you have all your bases covered. You'll also have and Every Day Carry, and EDC, which we'll talk about later. You'll also want to go through your bag about every three months or so to make sure everything is working the way it's supposed to, and to add or subtract any items that you need or no longer need as you educate yourself on survival techniques.

Don't get carried away with all the "what-if's", it's impossible to cover every single what-if you might encounter. If you fully covered every what-if you would need a truck load of supplies with you! All you have to be concerned with is your security, and keeping yourself warm, dry, and fed.

I don't fully agree with "Tiers" or "Levels" you might read about when studying Get Home Bags. Tiers and levels determine what you pack in your GHB according to how far you have to travel. It sounds good on the surface, and it is a good starting point, but there is more to consider than just the distance you must travel. These tiers vary depending on who authored them but they are pretty much as follows; Tier level-1; 1 to 3 hour walk, Tier level-2; 4 to 8 hours, and Tier level-3; Overnight. These prescribed tiers speculate that everyone is going to be traveling in the same terrain and climate. If you were traveling in the Northeast United States in the spring or fall, on flat level ground, or better yet, downhill all the way home, tiers would be great! But not everyone will be doing this, some of us might have to travel three hours in 10° weather and over hilly rocky terrain. According to the aforementioned Tier level mindset the recommended tier level for a 3 hour walk home is Tier level-1, but in this extreme scenario you better have packed a Tier level-3! Always plan for an overnighter!

What if the SHTF in a late summer morning, the temperature is already 85° with 70% humidity and you have a 15 mile walk ahead of you? Unless your 19 years old and just out of boot camp don't try to walk it! Find a safe place to wait it out until evening when it cools down, and use that time to go through your things and get yourself ready for your walk. But you know yourself and your capabilities, I don't, the final decisions you make are yours alone. Even if you're only one mile from home when the SHTF, a lot can happen in that twenty-or-so-minute walk; have the means to shelter yourself from a cold, rainy night. You can get hypothermia even in the summer time, you have to keep yourself warm and dry in all four seasons. If you are laying low for a few hours or so before your walk home, that would be a good time to plan your journey and go over your gear and keep yourself hydrated. You don't want to start on a long walk if you're not fully hydrated.

Q: What kind of backpack should I get?

A: One that all your stuff fits into.

There are so many different kinds of bags available it would be impossible to cover every option. You can get a hiking pack, a camping pack, or a military style pack. I favor the military style packs because they're built to take abuse, and the new style ones have all the MOLLE webbing that makes it easy to attach things to the outside, just about anywhere you want.

Some people say you should get a pack that "fits in" so you don't look out of place. This is what's called the "Grey Man", where you look inconspicuous. I'm not a proponent of the "Grey Man" mindset. The grey man is someone who blends in and looks inconspicuous as if he doesn't have a backpack full of equipment. This is really hard to achieve, especially while you're trying to look inconspicuous while humping a backpack full of equipment. It really makes no difference what backpack you use; people are going to know you have stuff inside whether you use a hiking pack or a high end military pack. What you really want is to look like someone that nobody wants to screw around with. Look strong, dedicated and unapproachable. People, or should I say cowards, who want to rob other people always look for easy targets; don't look like an easy target. I think a Ranger Green or Desert Tan MOLLE pack looks more intimidating than a neon green or orange hiking pack.

When packing your GHB remember to put heavier items toward the top of your pack. The backpack is on your back and is not in line with your natural center line. If the heavier items are at the top of the pack you don't have to lean as far forward to achieve center-of-gravity. Another thing to consider if you're going to be far from home is to store a folding wagon in your automobile (see figure 1). Not only can you carry your GHB in it, but anything else you might find can go in the wagon, and you can wheel it behind you. Have your GHB ready to grab-and-go in case you have to abandon your wagon in a hurry. If you don't have a wagon you can commandeer a shopping cart from a supermarket to wheel your stuff and give your back a break. You'll also burn less calories and get less dehydrated wheeling your supplies behind you rather than carrying them on your back. Of course if you have to traverse the wilderness or over rocky terrain the shopping cart isn't going to work, however, the wagon might work in the wilderness to a certain extent.

If it snows a lot in your area you might want to consider snowshoes and a toboggan instead of a wagon.

Figure 1- Folding Wagon

Knowledge

Knowledge is the most important thing you can have. You have to keep yourself educated in relevant SHTF subjects. Read survival manuals, military manuals, take courses in first aid, homesteading or anything else you think might help you keep yourself and your family comfortable in stressful times.

Learn about edible plants and insects in your area and any area you travel through, and learn how to prepare them for eating. Crickets and dandelions are very abundant where I live and they're both easy to prepare. Here in the northeast I can also eat clover flowers, but in the south those same flowers are poisonous, this is knowledge.

I find it easier to study one aspect of a subject at a time instead of trying to digest everything as a whole. Like edible plants and wildlife; study one edible plant or insect at a time. Reading a book about edible plants is overwhelming, but if you dedicate a full week or two and study just one thing, like dandelions, acorns, or cattails, and learn everything there is to know about eating that one item it will stick with you more than if you read about it in a book, then read about another plant 10 minutes later in the next chapter.

This book is by no means the final word on anything it covers, no book is. Highlight, underline, and take notes, and use these notes for further study.

You'll notice as you read further through this book that I never recommend expensive, state-of-the-art gadgets or equipment (except knives). I don't believe in them, and I also can't afford them. Being prepared isn't about buying new and expensive gear; it's preparing your mind so you can do the best with of what you have, and what you can afford.

Figure 2- Knowledge is gained through study.

Situational Awareness

Situational Awareness in knowing what's going on around you; who is where, how are they acting, are they a threat, and if so, are they a direct threat to you or a loved one? This is a very basic summary but it should give you an idea of what you should look for. Never be fully relaxed, always realize that something can happen at any given time.

Recognizing Threats

Q: How do you recognize a potential threat, someone who is up to no good? A: Treat everyone and everything as a potential threat.

You might be very surprised what seemingly normal people are capable of; an *"injured"* child, alone, on the side of the road. This is a good set-up for an ambush. A man walking with a limp and a cane, then when he gets close enough to you, he loses his limp and cracks you across the skull with his solid oak stick! Threats come in all shapes and sizes, be careful of stray dogs, they're hungry.

Don't trust anyone, when someone approaches you place your hand on your firearm; raise your other hand in a HALT gesture, while they are beyond 7 yards away. (see *The Tueller Drill* under *Security* in *The Get Home Bag; Your GHB* section.)

Eyeball people if you're in a group. Don't stare them down like you're looking for a fight, just examine them. Look at their faces and body language, trust your intuition. If everyone in the group has the look of despair and worry on their face and you see someone that stands out differently, keep your eye on him. He may be up to no good, or he just might be confident, prepared, and determined, just like you!

Binoculars: I have a small, lightweight pair of binos in my GHB so I can scan the road or path ahead and scope out potential dangers. If you are traveling by road you should check out every bridge you have to cross over and every overpass you have to pass under before you get to it. Bridges and overpasses are perfect ambush points for the bad guys.

Another obstacle to avoid are highways that have those Sound Barrier Walls constructed on either side of the highway. If you enter inside an area like this you only have two directions you can go, forward or backward, and it's easy for people that mean you harm to take advantage of this type of choke point.

The OODA Loop

The OODA Loop is a strategic tool developed by John Boyd, who was an Air Force fighter pilot during the Korean War. The OODA Loop is used to determine what your actions will be in any given situation. OODA stands for Observation, Orientation, Decision, and Action. On the surface these seem like very basic principles, but they can become very complex. We'll stick with the basics as it will take an entire book to get into every detail.

Observation: Boyd describes Observation as the collection of data by means of the senses.

Be alert, know what's going on all around you. Not only check the direction you're going but check to your left and right and what's behind you. We call this your flanks and your six. When you observe a bridge to pass over or under study it through your binos for a period of time. Keep looking to see if you notice any movement or anything out of the ordinary. I would suggest studying an area for at least fifteen minutes bare minimum, the longer the better.

If you're in the wilderness and all of a sudden birds fly out from the trees ahead of you, you can bet something or someone spooked them. Know what everything looks and sounds like in your surroundings and your environment. If you're resting at night to the sound of crickets and all of a sudden the crickets stop singing, it's for a very good reason. Tall grass sways in the breeze in a rhythmic pattern, if this pattern gets broken in a certain spot it's because something crawling within broke it. Watch your shadow; is it in front of you or behind you? If your shadow is front of you and suddenly there are two, that's not a good thing. If you're going around a corner and your shadow is in front of you it will give you away before you get to the corner, and vice versa; if you're approaching a corner and you notice somebody's shadow overcasting from the corner then you know someone else is there.

If you encounter someone who says they need help and they're crying, but with no tears, tell them you're sorry but you have to leave, and leave quickly.

Orientation: Boyd describes Orientation as the analysis and synthesis of data to form one's current mental perspective. Boyd referred to this this aspect of the OODA Loop as the Schwerpunkt, a German word used in Blitzkrieg Warfare that means Focal Point.

Your mental perspective includes *"Trusting your Gut"*. If you have a bad feeling about something it's most likely for a good reason. A good read about this concept is *The Gift of Fear: And Other Survival Signals That Protect Us from Violence* by Gavin de Becker. In it, Becker describes and give actual case studies where people have saved their own lives by trusting their gut feeling that something is about to go wrong.

Analyzing your situation is processing your observations to determine whether there is a threat or not. For example you're walking down the street and observe a group of people about three hundred yards down the road walking toward you. They appear to be two men, two women and two small children. You walk another twenty five yards, now the gap is closed by fifty yards, suddenly they cross the street to your side of the road. *Do they mean you harm?*

Decision: Boyd describes Decision as the determination of a course of action based on one's current mental perspective.

Now is time to decide if these people that just crossed the road to be on your side of the street mean you harm. You decide they probably don't because if they did they would have been a little sneakier about it. But you decide to avoid them anyway, even a friendly confrontation can turn dangerous fast in a SHTF situation.

Action: Boyd describes Action as the physical playing-out of decisions.

You decided to avoid confrontation with the group of people walking towards you. You are on a wooded country road and decide to cut right, and into the woods, when you're in the woods you move at a quicker pace to penetrate deeper into the forest. You get about fifty yards in and turn to around and realize you're in substantial cover of the forest. You then stop, remove your pack, get down and take out your handgun, then wait quietly listening to make sure no one entered the woods to follow you.

Fatigue

Fatigue is the slow loss of motor skills, the feeling of being tired and weakened from physical or mental stress. Fatigue can be relieved by periods of rest and proper rehydration. If you're feeling fatigued you need to rest

Morale

Morale is a person or group's feeling of confidence, enthusiasm, and discipline. Morale can be affected by doubt and anxiety. You have to be confident that you can and will rise above your situation and get yourself home. Doubt and negativity is the enemy of morale. You need to fix or separate yourself from any negativity. If you are with a loved one that is feeling anxiety or doubt you must reassure them that you have the experience, the means, and the resolve to keep everyone safe.

Figure 3- Inspirational reading is important for morale.

Keeping yourself as clean and as comfortable as possible will help with fatigue and morale. The simple act of washing yourself and brushing your teeth can work wonders. Inspirational reading also helps with morale. If you're religious you might want to have a pocket bible or whatever scripture relative to your beliefs; I carry a pocket version of the Elder Edda in my EDC. If you're not religious there are pocket versions of a lot of books available; Sailing Alone Around the World, SAS Survival Manual, and The Hobbit to name a few.

Work Kit GHB

The Work Kit is a GHB that has the supplies you need to get you home from your workplace. If you're very close to home, like a one or two hour walk for instance, it would probably be very small, maybe just covering the bare bones basics like a water filter, canteen, rain poncho, and a fire starter. If you work further from home you'll want to add an extra canteen, steel cup, mess kit, paracord and a tarp.

Car Kit GHB

The Cart Kit GHB is the one I'll be covering mostly in this book because it contains the most gear, at least mine does. If your need is only a Work Kit and your work is close to home you can very easily tailor everything discussed to fit your needs. On the other side of the coin if you work a great distance from home your Work Kit might have more gear than the average Car Kit.

The Car Kit is a GHB that spends its life in your vehicle. It should differ from your Work Kit GHB in that you don't know where or how far away from home you'll be when the SHTF. You could be at the store right around the corner from home, or several miles away. It should contain supplies you'll need to sustain yourself overnight, and under the most severe weather conditions.

Supplemental GHB

When the SHTF chances are you might not be alone, you might be with a friend or member of your family, or your entire family for that matter! I rarely see GHB's that take into consideration that the person might be with loved ones when the SHTF, this is where a Supplemental GHB comes in. It contains items that other people who might be with you will need. It's not an exact duplicate of your GHB, it supplements items the other person will need. Mostly personal items like a poncho, mess kit, hygiene kit, Knife, etc. A supplemental GHB can also be kept at work if you anticipate a coworker joining you on your walk home.

Specialized Equipment

Specialized Equipment is the supplies you'll need if you must travel a great distance or over rough terrain. This equipment can include climbing equipment, snake bite kit, specialized first aid items, etc. Specialized equipment needs specialized training, if you think you'll need gear like this get the proper training on how to use it.

When I mention "kits" in the following text, like "water kit" or fire kit", this doesn't mean that all components of the kit are stowed together in my GHB. They are sometimes scattered throughout different compartments in the bag.

Every Day Carry; Your EDC

A GHB should be used in conjunction with your Everyday Carry, what we refer to as your EDC. My EDC has some items in it that I don't have in my GHB, and some redundancy, especially fire. Aside from personal items that I use for work and for my daily routine, my EDC contains a compass, a flashlight, a ferrocerium rod (ferro rod), a small water stone, a Pilot's Survival Knife, a water key, a p-51 can opener, a FRED can opener, a Colt 1911, and four spare magazines (or a 5-shot .38 Snub Nose Revolver with 4 speed loaders). The bag itself is a Maxpedition Noatak Gearslinger. I carry my EDC everywhere I go. My youngest daughter reminds me when we go somewhere, "Don't forget your EDC, Daddy!" My kids are comfortable around guns and knives. I let them see them, I let them handle them, and I teach them to have respect for them. By being around weapons they have no curiosity about them so there is no reason to "play" with them like kids who are sheltered from such things tend to do. I explained to my kids that there are three basic rules of life:

"All knives are sharp, all guns are loaded and all people are stupid."

Follow these three rules and you will rarely get hurt.

Not included in my EDC bag is my folding pocket knife, a Gerber Applegate-Fairbairn Covert (see figure 4). I always carry a pocket knife and I've been carrying one since I was around seven years old. I remember when I was just about that age my father gave me a small, a very small, pocket knife. But in my little hands it was huge! After using it I felt it was too dull so I asked my father if he could sharpen it for me. My mother said "No!", but he sharpened it anyway, he said a dull knife is more dangerous. I watched in amazement while my father worked his magic on the oil stone. I loved watching my father sharpen knives, but then again

I loved watching my father do everything. After stropping this little knife on the stone at lightning speed he checked it with his thumb, then sliced a sheet of paper with it. He folded it up and handed it back to me. My mother said "He's going to cut himself with that thing!" My father's reply was, "Yes, he probably will." I took my knife and ran out of the house with an ear to ear grin! I just about always had a pocket knife with me from that day forward.

Figure 4- Applegate Fairbairn Covert Folder

I also carry a small pocket flashlight, it's a Bushnell Pro 100L High-Performance Flashlight, it uses two "AAA" batteries, is 100 lumens, and will last 3 ½ hours.

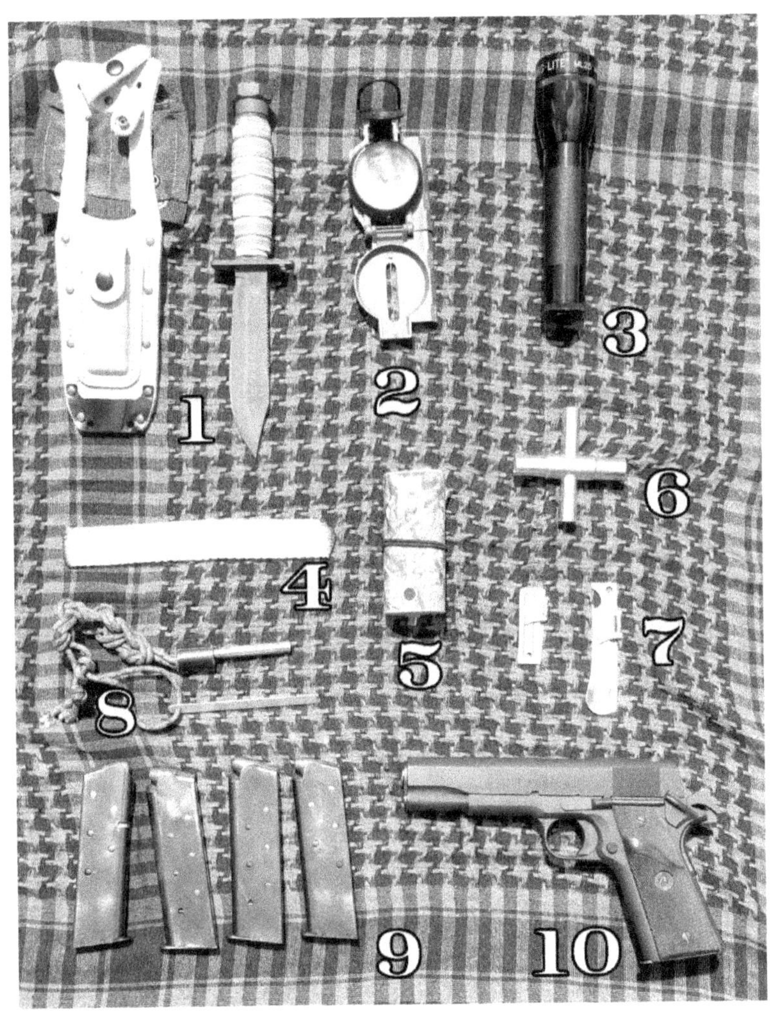

**Figure 5: Contents of my Maxpedition EDC

1- Pilot's Survival knife: Ontario Knife Company-Pilot's Survival Knife

2- Military Style Lensatic Compass

3- Maglight: A 2-C cell LED Maglite. The good thing about Maglites is that they are water proof and virtually indestructible. And their aluminum body can be used to beat someone's head in, in an emergency of course.

4- Charred wick: A Charred wick is a lantern wick with both ends burned and put out by smothering. The charred ends can catch a spark from a flint-and-steel or a ferro-rod. After it catches the spark, blow on it to get it smoldering. It can then be used to ignite a campfire.

5- Portable Power Charger

6- Water Key: This is a four way water key used to open water spigots on commercial buildings, apartment building, schools, etc.

7- P-51 and FRED Can Opener: The old fashioned way to open a can of food. FRED comes from the Australian Defense Force and stands for Field Ration Eating Device

8- Ferro-Rod: My ferro-rod has a length of paracord attached to it, and a broken piece of hacksaw blade to use as a sparker.

9 & 10- Colt 1911 and 4 Spare Magazines: My choice of sidearm is the ol' reliable 1911 style pistol in .45 caliber. I'm just an old fashioned type of guy. And when a Colt 1911 is empty you can use it to crack someone across the face.

Cash is another good thing to carry with you. If there is no electricity stores might still be opened for a few hours in hopes the lights come back on. If they are opened they will only be accepting cash.

Figure 6: Maxpedition Noatak Gearslinger

This is my EDC bag, Maxpedition Noatak Gearslinger in foliage. It's small, compact, and very durable. It's a sling bag so it has one strap that crosses over your chest. It's designed for concealed carry and can be fitted with a Velcro holster. The bag can be swung under your arm to wear in front to give quick access to all the compartments. Maxpedition is a high end bag but worth every penny.

The Get Home Bag; Your GHB

Water Kit

Water is the most important thing to have so we'll talk about this first. You have to have plenty of clean drinking water available if you are traveling far in hot weather. My water kit includes a Sillcock, also called a 4-way water key, a water filter, two 1-quart plastic military canteens, a steel canteen cup, coffee filters, and a collapsible bucket. You can read about the sillcock in the *City and Suburban* section under the *Terrain* heading.

Go online to Google Maps, or get a topographic map that shows waterways and map out potential water sources like rivers, lakes, and ponds, especially if you have a long walk home. Print these maps out and store them in a plastic bag inside your GHB. Studying these maps you will probably discover water resources that you didn't even know were there. By using Google Maps you can even see into backyards and find out who has a swimming pool. Make sure it's not a Salt Water Pool, you can't drink salinated water. Chlorinated pool water is drinkable but you have to let the water sit to release the chlorine, and then filter it. Chlorine evaporates faster than water, but you will have to let it sit in an opened container for a full 24 hours, or you can boil it for 15 minutes. Let it cool down and smell it to make sure it doesn't smell of chlorine. Be careful getting pool water, people might not like you in their backyards stealing water from their swimming pools without permission.

Water filters

Water filters are rated according to micron size. The most common emergency filters are 0.1 microns which filter out everything except viruses, which can be killed by boiling. You actually don't need a water filter; if you're boiling the water it's redundant to use a filter, and if you have to remove particles from the water a coffee filter will do the job. With that being said, I do use a water filter because I feel that there are too many pollutants that contaminate water, there is even pollution in the atmosphere that can contaminate rain water and a coffee filter and boiling will not filter this pollution out.

You have to take care of your water filter; if you use the Sawyer Mini remember to back flush it after each use, and in freezing cold weather a used water filter should be carried in one of your pockets close to your body to keep it from freezing. Water stays inside the filter and if it freezes the ice will expand and ruin your filter.

One thing that filters or chemical treatment of water does not do is remove any foul taste that is in the water. It might taste like crap after treatment but it's still safe to drink.

Coffee Filters

Coffee filters are used to filter out larger debris like leaves, dirt, and bugs prior to using a filtering device or before boiling.

Bleach disinfecting

Add 2 drops of pure bleach per quart of water. Stir the bleach into the water and let it stand for 30 minutes. This small amount of bleach will not hurt you; how many times have you swallowed chlorinated pool water? It's the same thing, but pool water contains even more bleach. Also bleach evaporates faster than water; I would let it sit covered for 30 minutes so the bleach doesn't evaporate before it gets a chance to kill all the bad stuff.

Iodine Treatment

Some precautions should be observed when using iodine to purify drinking water. If you are allergic to iodine don't use it, this is pretty much common sense. Most people allergic to shell fish are also allergic to iodine. Also if you have a thyroid problem, are on lithium, are a women over fifty, or are pregnant, you should not use iodine for water purification.

You can use 2% Tincture of Iodine to purify water by adding 5 drops per quart if the water is clear, if the water is cloudy add 10 drops per quart. Iodine should always be stored in a dark bottle because it is light sensitive

Water Purification Tablets

Water purification tablets contain iodine, chlorine or chlorine dioxide. These chemicals kill parasites, viruses, and bacteria that are commonly found in contaminated water. With these tablets colder water needs to be purified for a longer time, completely read and follow the directions on the bottle.

Gathering Water

A collapsible bucket (see figure 9) is great for catching rain water or scooping a large quantity or water from its source. It folds flat and is very lightweight. A water key is used to retrieve water from commercial buildings that have no handles on their water spigots; canteens and water bottles can be filled directly from spigots. In certain situations water that is taken from a spigot should still be filtered and boiled

In my water kit I use a Sawyer Products Mini Water Filtration System. I store it inside two water bottles; one has its top cut off so it can be used as a receptacle, the other has its bottom cut off so it can be used as a funnel (see figure 7). The good feature of this filter is that a water bottle can be screwed onto the filter, so I can screw the funnel piece onto the filter and hang it up so it will work as a drip filter, catching the clean water in the receptacle (see figure 8). This filter also has a straw attachment so it can be used to drink directly from the source. And it has a cleaning plunger device that can also be used to suck water out of the source and into a receptacle. If the water is dirty or muddy it should first be filtered through a coffee filter to remove the larger impurities.

The steel canteen cup can be used to boil water to remove smaller impurities like viruses. Water should be boiled for a full three minutes at a rapid boil. Let the water cool then shake it to aerate it to improve its taste. When the weather is wet and you can't find suitable wood to build a fire, this is where an Esbit stove will come in handy. A 14-gram Esbit tablet will burn for about 12 minutes at about 1300°F. Do not use a double walled stainless steel container to boil water! Use only a single walled container! If you attempt to boil water in a double walled container it will explode! Use only single walled, metal containers to boil water in.

Figure 7: Water Kit; From left clockwise; Coffee filters, 1.5 liter funnel bottle, 1 liter receptacle bottle, Sawyer Mini Filter, Straw attachment, Cleaning plunger, Squeezable water bottle.

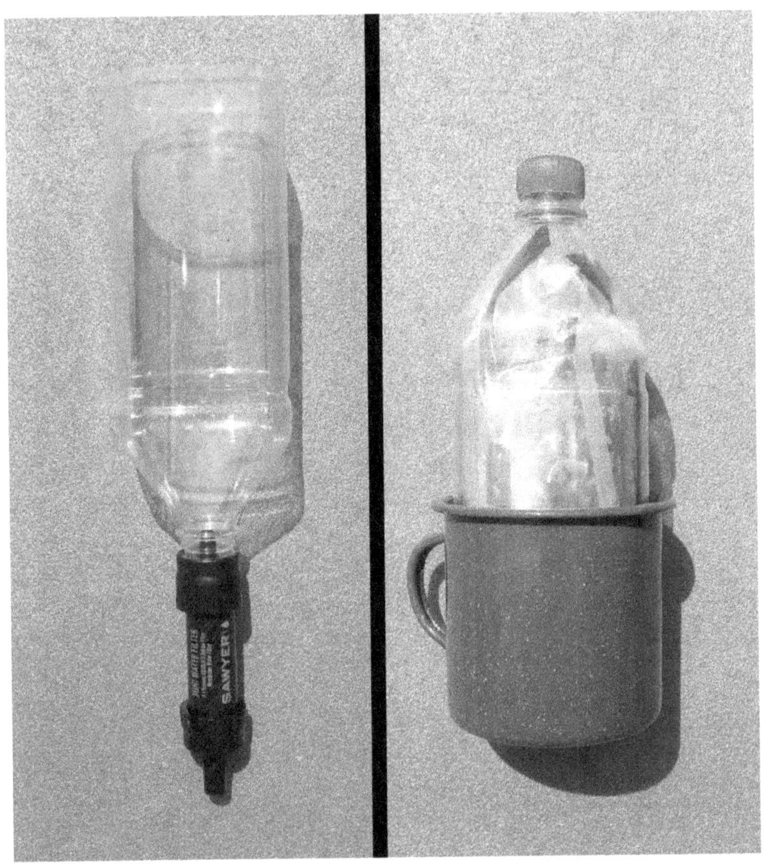

Figure 8: Set up for drip filtration and packed up for
storage.

Figure 9- Collapsible Water Bucket

Mess Kit and Food

Mess Kits

Mess kits can be made from steel or aluminum. You can purchase a mess kit in which each component stores within itself, or you can piece one together for yourself. A stainless steel pie plate makes an excellent dinner plate. I use an enameled steel pie plate. You can use cake pans as well. The benefit of having a steel plate is that you can cook on it and eat off it too. There is no need for a separate cooking pan.

A steel cup is a must for your mess kit. Once again, you can use a steel cup to cook in or boil water for purification.

I have metal utensils made for camping use. You can get plastic or metal, the choice is yours. I used to use plastic utensils, but I quickly found out the benefit of metal utensils is that you can use them to cook with and don't have to worry about them melting from the heat.

Food

In times of distress hunger is sometimes forgotten, this is why people suffering from severe depression don't eat. If this happens to you in a SHTF situation you still must eat. A lot of us have plenty of stored energy (fat), so we can afford to go without food for a while. If you don't eat for more than 24 hours you need to eat something, even if it's a small meal or snack. I know you can go three weeks without food before you die, but the final two and a half weeks of that three weeks period is the time you wish you were dead.

You need fat, protein, and carbs to keep yourself going. Nuts, jerky, peanut butter, are a few things that offer these nutrients. If you stubbornly adhere to weird, unnatural diets you'll soon be dead in a SHTF situation.

You can throw a few military MRE's in your pack or some cans of soup, spam, or whatever. If your bag is stored in your car, in the summer canned food and MRE's will spoil really fast from the heat. The inside of a car can reach over 140° in some areas. An MRE will only last one month at 120°, compare that to 48 months at 60° and five years at 50°. According to the FDA temperatures over 100° are harmful to canned foods. Freezing is also bad for MRE's and canned food. The expansion of the contents can damage the packaging and spoil the food. None of this food storage should be a problem for your Work Kit GHB as you'll most likely be keeping it within a temperature controlled environment.

When purchasing MRE's make sure you buy the brands that are made by one of the three Military manufacturers, these are; Ameriqual, Sopakco, and The Wornick Company. The Commercial brand names for MRE's from these companies are A Pack from Ameriqual, Sure-Pak from Sopakco, and Eversafe from Wornick. Although these companies are the suppliers of MRE's to the Military, their civilian versions differ from the Military versions. The Military versions have more food per MRE and more of a variety of entrees, desserts, and other components.

When you carry MRE's it's a good idea to strip them down, which is to open the packaging and remove components that you don't need. For example you can remove the creamer, the sugar packs, or the candy, and trash any cardboard packaging. If you feel like you need the creamer and candy, then keep it! After you strip it down repack it back in the plastic package, or repackage it in a gallon zip baggie, then stow it in your backpack. Everyone has their own idea of how to strip down an MRE and repack it, there is no right or wrong way to do it.

If your walk is only going to be a few hours you really don't have to worry about food, at least not a meal. Protein or granola bars would do just fine. You can also eat CRAP. CRAP stands for chocolate, raisins, almonds, and peanuts. Mix equal amounts of each and keep it in a one gallon zip bag. Or you can mix any concoction you like. Learning about edible plants in your area is also a good idea. Learn about plants that do not require a lot of preparation; one that you can just grab and eat raw.

In my preps I do what I like to call "The Prepper's Quarter." You heard of the baker's dozen? That's 13 instead of 12. The prepper's quarter is for every three months of food I store, I store additional month. So four months of food is in reality only three months, four days food is three days. So if I inventory four months of MRE's, I consider it only three months worth of food. I do this for any unforeseen events that might occur, prepping within your preps, so to speak. I might need to house a friend and account for another mouth to feed, some food might go bad, or I might have to trade some food for something else I need. I know this has nothing to do with what we're talking about, but I wanted to mention it anyway. When I did construction work we always added 10% waste when we figured out the materials that were needed to complete the job. This covered damage, or something we didn't consider, or any other unforeseen event. This goes with preparing as well, there's a saying in the preparedness community: two is one and one is none. Things break, get lost, or good ol' Murphy steps in and does his thing.

Insects

Many insects are edible and are a very rich source of protein.

Crickets and Grasshoppers are very rich in protein and can be found pretty much everywhere except cold climates. You can find crickets hiding under logs, rocks, and debris. You can catch them easily by hand, but they are fast!

To prepare crickets and grasshoppers dry roast them in a pan, or skewer them and roast over flame. You can even sauté them in olive oil with a little garlic, but you probably won't have olive oil or garlic with you so stick to dry roasting them, or sauté them in a little water and sprinkle on some Old Bay. You can eat the entire bug if you want, but a lot of people like to pull their legs and head off. However you eat or prepare them, always make sure to cook crickets and grasshoppers thoroughly to reduce the risk of parasite transmission.

Termites can be dry roasted in a pan just like crickets, and are less likely to carry parasites than all other insects.

Wood Lice, also known as potato bugs, pill bugs, and roly-polies can be found in the same places as crickets. Catch them and boil them. Make sure they're boiled thoroughly, 3 to 5 minutes at a rapid boil.

Cooking

Some MRE's come with a chemical heater so you can heat the food up without giving away your position, a fire can be seen for miles. If you have canned food or just caught yourself a squirrel, you can cook it up over a campfire. Speaking of catching a squirrel, it might be a good idea to pack some salt and pepper, Old Bay, or some other kind of seasoning. Who says you can't eat gourmet when the SHTF?

You can cook over an open fire or use an Esbit Stove if an open fire isn't safe or feesable. Esbit stoves work great and use their own fuel tabs to work. You can also use burning coals from your fire in an Esbit stove. They're good for heating canned food or boiling water but not really for preparing a gourmet meal. The main reason I carry one in my GHB is to quickly disinfect water or to cook a quick meal when a larger fire isn't feasible.

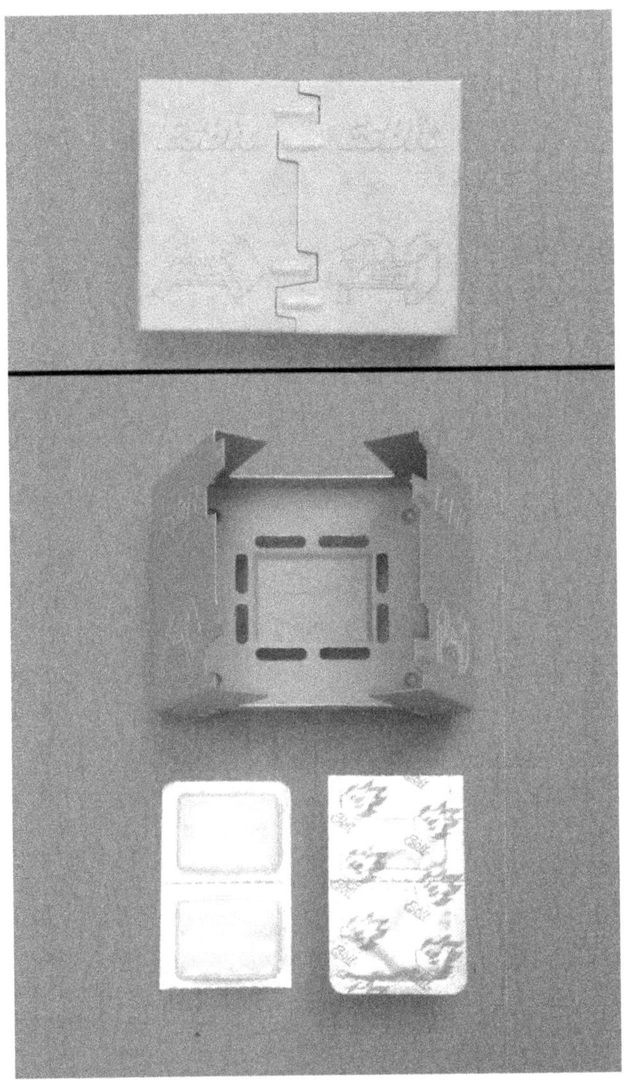

Figure 10: Esbit Stove

Figure 11: Mess Kit; Enameled Steel pie plate, Enameled steel cup, and Plastic utensils.

Fire Kit

Fire is just as important as food and water. Fire is used in every aspect of survival. It cooks our food, sterilizes our water, and keeps us warm. There are many various ways to build a fire and your kit should have three different options available to you.

Fire Ignition

Storm Matches: Storm Matches are long wooden matches that have thick a sulphur covering about half to two thirds the length of the match (see figure 12). They are also called Lifeboat Matches. When you light them the sulphur burns for a few seconds and is virtually windproof. If it's not an emergency to get a fire going DO NOT waste your matches; use them only as a last resort. Try to build a fire the "hard way" first. Don't try to light a fire with a battery and steel wool. It works but it drains the entire battery.

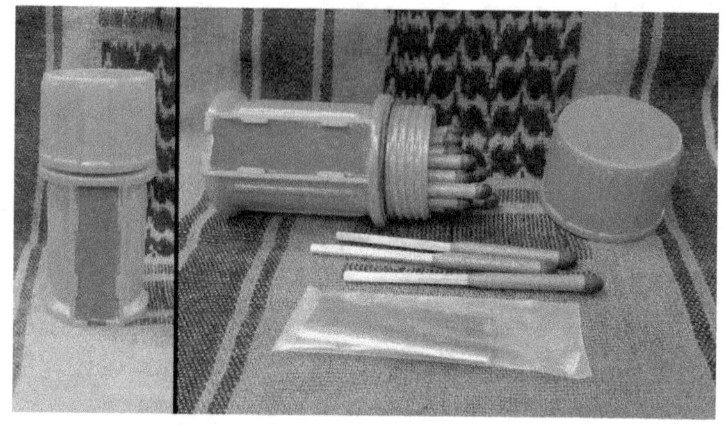

Figure 12- Storm or Lifeboat Matches

Ferrocerium Rod: Also known as a Ferro Rod, this is a man-made metal material that you scrape with the edge of your knife or a piece of steel and it produces sparks at temperatures reaching 5,430°! The sparks are aimed at a dry fire starting medium such as grass, charred cloth, or a charred wick.

Flint and Steel: The old fashioned way of starting a fire, a sharp piece of flint is struck with a hardened piece of high carbon steel. The sharp edge or the flint actually shears bits of steel from the striker which ignite to cause sparks. It takes a little practice to use a flint and steel but it's easy once you get the hang of it. The trick is to have a sharp edge on the flint.

Magnifying Glass: A magnifying glass can be used to start a fire by concentrating the sunlight onto dry fire starting medium. Most everyone did this when they were a kid. The only drawback is you can only do this on a sunny day.

Lighter: Everyone knows how to start a fire with a lighter. Use a disposable lighter, refillable lighters leak their fluid and they dry out and might not work when you really need them.

Fire Medium

Wet Fire: Wet fire cubes are similar to Esbit Fuel but they don't burn as hot. You can't cook with them but they do serve their purpose of starting a fire. To use a wet fire cube: Shave a few slivers off of one and place them on top of the cube. Use a ferro rod to shoot sparks at the slivers and it should light. (Esbit fuel will not light with sparks, you need a flame to ignite them.) It will burn for a few minutes after it's lit.

I also carry a Pencil Sharpener (see figure 13), most of the time anyway. It's a quality brass sharpener that has two holes to accommodate fat and regular pencils. It works well for making shavings for kindling. All you do is find some twigs that fit in the respective holes and sharpen them. The shavings you create are used for kindle. You can also use a pencil sharpener as a tool to make points on sticks to trap and kill small animals.

Figure 13- Pencil Sharpener

Charred Cloth: Charred cloth is cloth that has been burned in a closed metal container in which the lack of oxygen keeps the cloth from turning to ash; it becomes a cloth charcoal and is very fragile. When a hot spark comes in contact with the charred cloth it will smolder like charcoal. This smoldering cloth can then be placed in a handful of dry grass, and will ignite if you gently blow on it.

To make Charcloth you need a small metal container with a separate lid. a hinged lid is fine but a separate lid is better. Make a small hole in the lid with a fat sewing needle or the point of a thin finishing nail. The hole shouldn't be too big, a small hole is all you need. If you're using one with a hinged lid you don't have to make the pinhole in it, there are already holes by the hinge. Cut some small squares, roughly 1"x 1", of cotton cloth from old tee shirts, they must be 100% cotton, hemp, or any other natural material, no synthetics. Close the lid and place it on a smoldering log or on your stove top, you'll start to see smoke coming through the hole. You can remove it from the heat source after a few minutes, the cloth will continue to burn inside. When to smoke stops coming out its done, let it cool and open it up and you should have black pieces of charred cloth. They are fragile but you will be able to handle them without a problem. When these pieces of charred cloth catch a spark they will instantly smolder, you can keep the smoldering going by gently blowing on it. You just made fire.

Charred Wick: Works the same way as charred cloth. This is simply a new, dry wick to a kerosene lamp that has the ends charred. To make a charred wick ignite the end of the wick, let it burn for a few seconds and smother it out. Keep it in your fire kit and make sure it stays dry. To use it catch a spark on the charred end and blow on it, it will smolder like that for hours if you let it. Use it like the charred cloth to ignite a loose bundle of dry grass then extinguish the wick by smothering it out. The wick can be used over and over again.

Fuzz Stick: A Fuzz Stick is good for kindling because the "fuzz" ignites faster and easier than a solid piece of wood. You make a fuzz stick by taking a piece of firewood about wrist thick and carving slivers on it. Hold the stick on a steady surface like a sturdy log. Start about three inches from the bottom and carve a sliver of wood, but don't carve it off, stop so that it curls down and stop. Do this around the whole piece of wood, then move up another three inches and do it again, and so on. When your done you'll end up with a fuzzy stick.

Building a Fire

When you use a fire for warmth, your body burns fewer calories for heat and you therefore require less food to keep yourself going. A good fire to is also a great morale booster, and the smoke of a fire repels insects.

A fire needs three elements to burn, these are: fuel, heat, and oxygen.

The three types of fuel used in building a fire are tinder, kindling, and fuel. Try to avoid building a large fire, build as small a fire as possible. A smaller fire requires less fuel so you don't have to gather as much wood.

Before you build a fire you need to gather all of the fuel elements together. Place some tinder material in your fire area, and then add some kindling over it. Make everything loose and airy so oxygen can get to the fire easily. Fresh cut green wood is difficult to ignite, when gathering wood look for dead, standing, leaning, or fallen trees with branches that are not touching the ground. Wood that is in contact with the ground is usually wet or rotted.

Tinder: Tinder is easily ignited with a minimum of heat, such as from a spark from your ferro rod or a glow on your charred wick. Tinder should be fine, dry wood shavings or dry grass. You can use a pencil sharpener to create shavings from dry twigs. If you're traveling a far distance you might want to gather tinder material and store it in your pack before you set off on your journey.

If you're using a match or lighter you can just light the tinder at this point. If you're using a sparking method like a ferro rod you should create a loose nest out of your dry grass, get a spark in there and gently blow on it to get it smoldering. Do this close to your fire area because when it bursts into flame you add it into the fire material you have set up. Get it burning by adding some thin kindling to it to get it going.

Kindling: Kindling material should be dead, dry twigs and sticks up to about the thickness of your finger.

The kindling wood is placed over the tinder and arranged so that it ignites by the flames of the burning tinder, don't pack a lot of sticks on the tinder, you want a few spaced apart. Use thinner kindling at first then add thicker material as it gets burning. When you get the thicker kindling burning good, you can add larger fuel material to the fire.

Fuel: Fuel wood is the thicker pieces of wood. You can split the wood from dead, dry, thicker branches. Fuel wood doesn't have to be completely dry as long as your fire burning good. Wet wood produces more smoke so keep that in mind. Hardwood will provide more heat than softer woods, like pine. But pine wood ignites more easily than hardwood, but also burns a lot faster.

Splitting Wood

You can split wood with your knife by a method called Batoning, pronounced buh-tahn-ing. It's called batoning because you use a stick as a baton to whack the knife through the wood. To do this, cut a piece of fire wood about ten to fourteen inches long and about as thick as your wrist. Get another piece of sturdy wood about eighteen inches long, this will be your baton. Place one end of the fire wood on a sturdy surface like a stone or a log, then put edge of the knife on the top end of the fire wood as if you're going to split it, make sure a good portion of the point hangs over the edge. Tap the back edge of your knife with your baton until it penetrates the wood, now start whacking the protruding point to drive the knife down and split the wood. That's all there is to it. If you're afraid your knife will break, don't worry, it won't, unless you're using a fighting knife or a cheap piece of shit. Never baton wood with a knife designed strictly for fighting.

I should also mention a small folding saw comes in handy for processing wood instead of trying to break it over your knee. There are many different brands including the Bahco Laplander, the Silky Gomboy, EverSaw, I use an Ozark Trail that cost under $10.00.

Dakota Fire Hole

A Dakota Fire Hole is good to use if you really need a fire and security is a priority, this method conceals the fire completely underground. To build a Dakota Fire Hole dig a round hole about 12 inches in diameter and 12 to 16 inches deep, then dig another hole the same diameter about 18 inches away from the first hole. This second hole can be dug at an angle toward the first hole, then when you reach the same depth tunnel into the first hole. Now when you build a fire in the first hole it will such the air it needs to burn through the second, very similar in concept to a Rocket Stove.

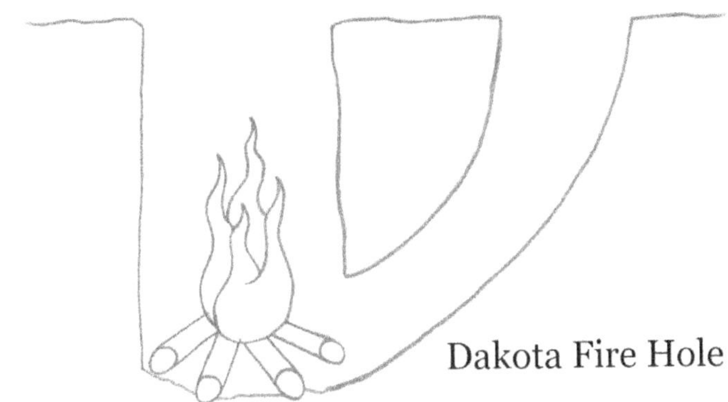

Dakota Fire Hole

Figure 14- Folding saw

Hygiene Kit

Hygiene is important, keeping yourself clean lowers the risk if sickness and infection. Cleaning yourself has a positive psychological effect as well, you'll feel more comfortable which will lower fatigue, relieve stress, and increase morale.

You must keep your hands clean especially after going to the bathroom. The most common gastrointestinal illness is from exposure to fecal-borne pathogens; after you wipe your ass, wash your hands! Cleaning your hands should be done immediately when you stop to rest.

Keeping clean includes brushing your teeth and taking care of your breath. Just because it's a SHTF scenario doesn't mean you have walk around smelling like a piece of shit. Think about it, what happens if you encounter a Damsel in Distress? Do you really want to smell like crap and have breath that can wake the dead?

Of course you'll need toilet paper for obvious reasons. And to clean yourself you should have two wash cloths, a small towel and travel size soap. You don't need a lot of water to clean yourself; this is another situation where a small collapsible bucket will come in handy. If you can, fill it with clean, filtered water and take a bird bath. Don't forget to get behind your ears. A little travel size deodorant and you're a new man, or woman! A hair brush or comb is always a good idea to have to complete your little birdbath. Once again, feeling clean and refreshed will decrease fatigue and increase morale.

A travel size tooth brushing kit comes next, along with some mouth wash. In a pinch you can even brush your teeth with mouthwash, it's better than nothing!

I know what you're thinking; *what if all this water is not available to use to clean yourself?* The answer is simple; then don't. Save what little water you have for drinking.

Shelter Kit

Shelter is anything that protects you from the elements, including your clothes. You not only have to be dressed for the conditions you are traveling in, you also need a complete change of clean, dry clothes. You always sleep in your clean dry clothes, and travel in your wet clothes. I get more into this in the Seasons and Weather Section. Speaking about dry clothes you should always have protection from the rain; a military grade poncho works real well. They cost more than the cheaper plastic or vinyl ponchos but are much more comfortable to wear.

Sleeping bags

You'll need a sleeping bag if the temperature will get below 65°. I carry a compact sleeping bag rated for 40°, which is overkill in the summer, but I feel that it's a good all-around sleeping bag for my region and if I'm inside with my coat on it keeps me protected at temperatures between 20° and

30°. I like the compact one for the obvious reason that it doesn't take up a lot of room, a full size sleeping bag takes up a lot of real estate. You want to insulate yourself from the ground if it is cold as a cold ground will drain heat from your body while you sleep. Sometimes a sleeping bag isn't enough, you should pack leaves underneath you as insulation, especially do this for children. A younger child should share a sleeping bag with one of their parents or an older sibling.

If you're in a region that experiences consistant cold weather below 30° you may want to consider getting a Military ECWS, Extreme Cold Weather System.

The U.S. Armed Forces Modular Sleep System, MSS, is the official name for the ECWS, the Extreme Cold Weather System. This is a four piece system that consists of a Green Patrol Bag, a Black Intermediate Bag, a Woodland Camouflage Waterproof Bivy Cover, and a Black Stuff Sack.

Each piece can be used alone or in conjunction with the other bags, when all the bags are used together the system is rated to -40 to -20 degrees. Of course the colder it is the less sleep time you'll get to enjoy, from what I understand the system is rated for a four hour sleep at -20 degrees.

The Patrol Bag alone is rated for warm climate use and protects you at temperatures between 30 and 50 degrees, The Intermediate Bag is rated for cold climate use and will protect you from temperatures ranging between -10 and 30 degrees. Using the Bivy Cover makes it a complete waterproof shelter.

Tarps

I carry two tarps in my GHB. One is a small 5x7, quality Emergency Blanket called a Grabber All Weather Blanket. This one has silver mylar on one side and a green color on the other. It has grommets on each corner so it can be used to make a small shelter. The other is a larger 8x10 Realtree camo pattern tarp that can be used to construct a larger shelter. Included in my shelter kit are six stainless steel tent spikes. These are the thin round type that has a small portion of one end bent at a 90° angle. These are light weight and take up hardly any room, they sit on the bottom of my pack and I don't even know they're there.

When building a tarp shelter remember to keep it small, a smaller shelter is easier to warm and you can actually warm an entire shelter with a candle. There are long burning candles available that will even burn for a few days! There is a 115 hour available candle that comes as a glass container with about 12 ounces of liquid paraffin wax. There's also a solid wax candle that will burn for 120 hours, and wax candles that come in resealable tin cans that are advertised to last anywhere between 24 and 50 hours. There are also long burning tea lights that will burn for 8 hours.

A good trick to use when building a tarp shelter is what George W. Jasper calls a Cobbler's Peg, and he demonstrates its use in his book *Six Ways in and Twelve Ways Out* (see figure 15). A Ridge Line is set up between two trees with paracord, The tarp is draped over a ridge line and the cord is pulled through the grommet and held in place with a stick. This works especially well when rigging the ridge line at an angle to set up your tarp as a tube tent style where the opening is larger than the rear, the tension will keep the tarp from sliding down.

Figure 15- A Cobbler's Peg

Cordage

Cordage is important to have in any survival situation. I carry 50 feet of paracord. Paracord comes in different colors, I usually have OD Green or some type of camouflage. I should mention here that I don't believe in having Bright Orange cord, emergency blankets or anything else that is *easy to see*. This might be good if you're hiking in the woods during normal times, but after the SHTF there will be no more normal times. The better you can hide when you have to, the better your chances are of survival. Now let's get back to cordage. You can also carry a spool of Bank Line in your GHB. Bank Line is tar coated cordage; the tar coating makes it tacky so when you tie a knot in it, it stays. Paracord is nylon and is slippery against itself, bank line doesn't slip. A Figure 9 Rope Tightener works hand in hand with cordage and shelter building. A Figure 9 will tighten, and secure ropes and cordage without knots.

Figure 16- A Figure 9 Rope Tightner.

Someone once pointed out that my paracord was not milspec 550 cord. *So what?* It doesn't matter if the cord is milspec 550 or not. Just make sure its good, strong cord. There should be a strength rating on the package. The cord I have is rated at 350 lbs. This is good enough for tying a tarp down in the rain.

Other Shelter Considerations

A quality Shemagh is good to have in your GHB. It's part of my Shelter Kit, not that I can build a shelter with one, but it can be used to shelter you from the sun. There are dozens of cool and fancy ways to tie one around your head, but if you just drape one over your head and hold it in place with a bandana or put a baseball hat over it, it will protect your head, your neck, and your shoulders from the sun. You won't look as tacticool as the other guy, but your shemagh will be serving its purpose.

Other things that are not really shelter but do protect you from the environment are Bug Repellant, a Cooling Towel, and Work Gloves. Bug Repellant is self-explanatory. The main ingredient in most insect repellants is a chemical called DEET. Rather than killing insects, DEET works by making it hard for them to smell you. DEET was developed by the U.S. Army around the mid 40's, and was registered for use by the public in the late

50's. When using DEET make sure you read and follow all directions and precautions on the product label. You're not supposed to apply DEET over cuts or wounds, and it's only for use on exposed skin. If you have children you should also carry a bug repellant that is safe for them to use; kids should use not more than 10% to 30% concentration of DEET. And never apply DEET to the hands or near eyes and mouth of children.

I mentioned a Cooling Towel elsewhere in this book, but I'll mention it again. I use a frogg toggs Chilly Pad Cooling Towel. A Cooling Towel works the same way sweat does, through evaporative cooling.

I carry Work Gloves also, a good pair of ordinary work gloves is good when you have to process wood for a camp fire, building a shelter, and navigating your way over a barbed wire fence. They also come in handy for grabbing hot cooking utensils, like your canteen cup or if you cook with a pie plate over a camp fire.

I have a few large Contractor Bags on the bottom of my pack. They have a lot of uses but I think the most important one is that they can be stuffed with leaves and use as an insulator from the cold ground.

Security Kit

A security kit is obviously what you use to protect yourself. My security items include an edged weapon, a firearm, and lighting devices. There are other items that are not obvious security items that can be used for protection, like a shovel.

Lighting

I include lighting as security because you have to be able to see a potential threat in order to identify it as one. I carry a small, two "C" cell Maglite in my EDC. It's small and light enough to carry yet big and heavy enough to crack someone across the face with, in an emergency. I also carry a two "AA" mini Maglite in my GHB as backup. I not a fan of those expensive high beam tactical flashlights, a Maglite is moderately priced and they have proven themselves for many years. They are not the brightest flashlights, especially compared to the high tech lights available today, but I feel they're the best in their price range. I choose my flashlights like I choose my girlfriends; dependable, long lasting, and not too bright.

In the picture above is a Luci Inflatable Solar Light. These lights are amazing! I keep one attached to the outside of my pack so it charges while I walk. It has three settings, low, bright, and strobe. It does take 7 hours to fully charge, but at full charge the light will last for 12 hours on the brightest setting. I rarely use the brightest setting, the low setting is fine. This light is waterproof and can handle temperatures between 15°to 122° F. I have a few of these lights, and the first one I purchased has been in my backyard all year round, in all four seasons for the past 3 years. It's been rained on, snowed on, and blown away and it still works fine! The plastic is thick and durable and has never gotten a hole in it. The light will work regardless, and it doesn't have to be inflated to use it.

Firearms

An entire book can be written on firearms, and whichever one you decide to carry is a personal preference. Some people like revolvers, some like compact automatics. Even the ammunition the gun takes varies a lot, 9mm, .45ACP, .40, .357, and .38 are some of the most popular.

My firearm of choice is a Colt 1911, .45 with a 7-round magazine. I sometimes carry a S&W Model 60, .38 Snub Nose Revolver. It's more comfortable and more concealable.

When I carry my Colt I carry four spare 7-round magazines for a total of 35 rounds ready to go, which I carry in my EDC bag. I also carry a spare 25 to 50 rounds of ammo in my GHB just in case. Also in GHB is an ALICE type web belt with a Bianchi M12 holster. (see figure 17) This is a military style flap holster that will serve its purpose in SHTF-Get-Home scenario. In most situations I would prefer to carry my firearm concealed, but I have the ALICE belt and holster if I need it. I attached MOLLE style magazine pouches to the pistol belt. (see figure 18) To do this, insert the MOLLE strap through the bottom webbing, then snap it down. Do this to all of them on the pouch. Then just thread the belt through the MOLLE straps. It's as simple as that! I only mention it because I had more than one person ask me how I attached a MOLLE pouch to a web belt. It's secure and won't go anywhere.

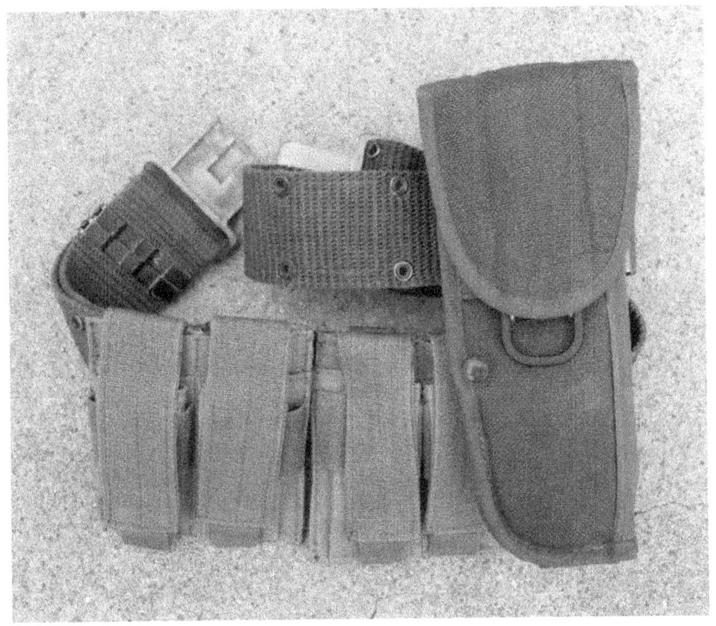

Figure 17- Bianchi M-12 Holster

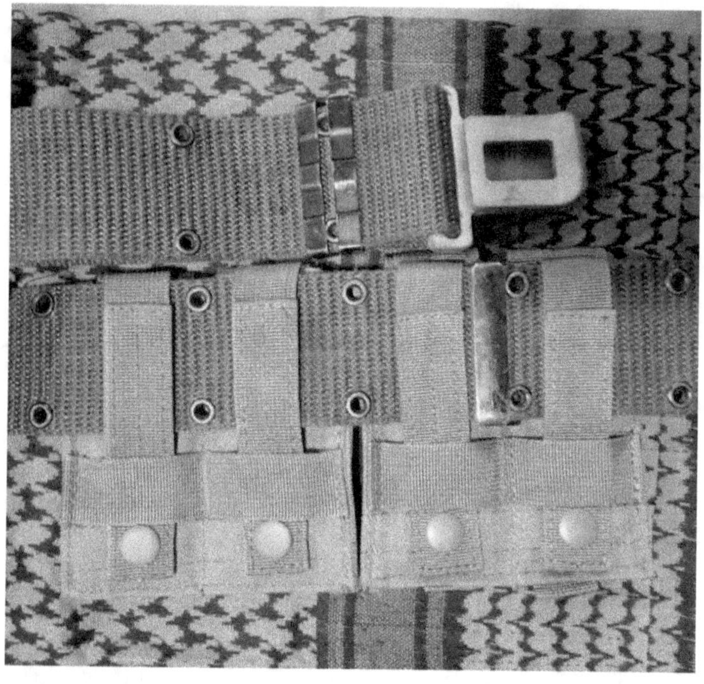

Figure 18- The back of the MOLLE straps set up for belt attachment.

When I carry my .38 S&W I keep four speed loaders in nylon pouches, with the five rounds in the chamber that's a total of 25 rounds. I can attach the speed loaders to my belt or keep them in a dump pouch attached to my belt.

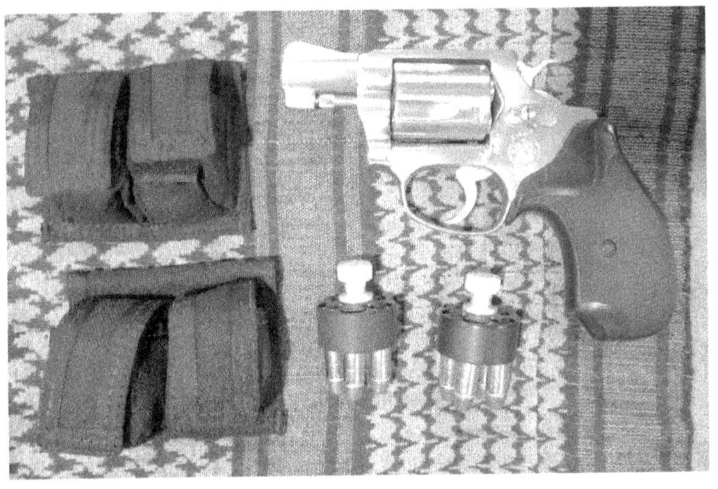

Figure 19- S&W Model 60

Before carrying a firearm be absolutely sure you are legally able to carry, laws vary by state and county. If you are unable to carry a firearm you might consider getting pepper spray or bear spray, and a stun gun, but in reality you should be carrying a firearm. There are takedown Lever Action Rifles available that breakdown and will fit in your pack. *"Lever Actions suck! What will I do with a Lever Action?"* More than you'll be able to do with nothing! A lever action rifle is better than throwing rocks. You can also build an AR15 from an 80% kit, or purchase a finished lower receiver from a gun shop and build one from there, cheaper and better than a lot of the rifles that are being sold today (see figure 20). There is no reason in America why you shouldn't own a firearm or why you shouldn't have one at least in your car if not on your person. I'm not condoning that anyone should break the law, but I will say that if you don't have the balls or wherewithal to arm yourself now you will not magically conjure up a pair of balls to arm yourself after the SHTF.

I only mention a total of four firearms here; but there are literally hundreds if not thousands of different firearms you can use to defend yourself, especially when you consider every configuration available. It will take an entire book to cover even a fraction of the firearms available, luckily for you one such book is available. It's called *Boston's Gun Bible*, by Boston T. Party, over 800 pages long. This book is currently out of print but you can find copies of it used at good prices.

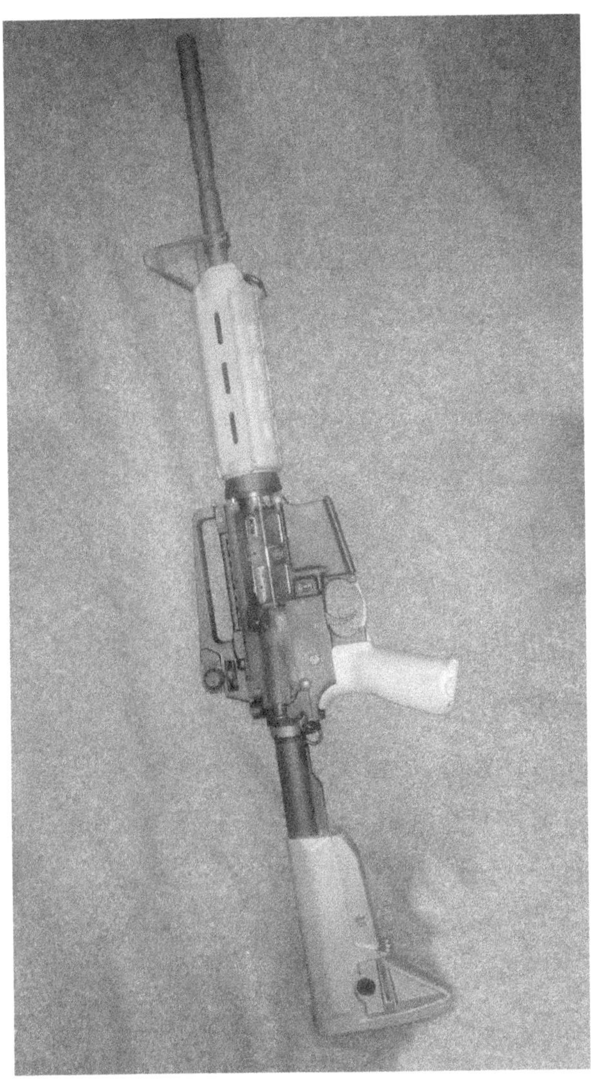

Figure 20-Home Built AR 15

The Tueller Drill

Sergeant Dennis Tueller of the Salt Lake City, Utah Police Department created a self-defense training exercise for police to prepare against a knife attack when armed with a holstered handgun. He first conducted a study of how quick an attacker with a knife could close in on an officer from a dead stop at 7 yards (21 feet) away. His tests determined that the average time an assailant could reach a target at this distance was within 1.5 seconds. These results were published in SWAT magazine in 1983 and a police training video titled, "How Close is Too Close?"

People started calling this the "21 foot rule", however Sgt. Tuller himself never used this term and denounces the idea of any such "rule". The "21 foot rule" gives the impression that an Officer will be justified in shooting a perpetrator armed with a knife at 21 feet. This way of thinking has many negative implications for a police officer.

What Tueller's Drill and experiment shows us is that we have to be aware of confrontations even at a distance of 7 yards away. A police officer trains to draw his gun and shoot from his holster which is located on his hip at the ready position, and with his training and preparedness he is still at risk of the bad guy getting on him from a distance of 7 yards. If you have your firearm concealed, and you're encumbered by wearing a backpack in a SHTF scenario, you're at an even a greater risk. Keep potential confrontations at a safe distance and keep your firearm in a ready position on your person.

Knives

Just like firearms, an entire book can be written on knives. The basic things you need to know about knives are the Grind, blade style, and quality of the steel. The knife's Tang should be considered as well. The tang is the part of the knife that's hidden under the handle.

The best knives are made from high carbon tool steel like A-2. Randall Knives and Blackjack Knives are made from tool steel. There are other companies that use tool steel as well; you have to do your research. It is hard to find a folder made from tool steel; my Gerber is made from 154CM which is a stainless steel but contains 1.05% carbon, which is considered a high carbon content. High carbon knives are strong and hold an edge very well.

My favorite edge is a traditional edge; commonly known as a "Convex Grind". You find this edge on

**Figure 21- Top: Convex Grind
Bottom: Scani Grind**

Randall knives and Blackjack Knives. Jeff White Knives also puts a convex grind on his Bush craft knives. A convex grind has a bevel on each side of the blade that is slightly rounded as they taper to form the edge. A "Scandinavian Grind" or "Scandi Grind" as it is commonly referred to, the blade tapers to the edge and then bevels to form the sharpened edge, much like a chisel.

Two knives that concern us here are Fighting knives and Survival/Bushcraft knives. A fighting knife's only intended purpose is for fighting. That means it will not make a good survival knife. It will break if you tried to chop or split wood with it. You can use a fighter for skinning and processing small game but it is not a survival knife.

A knife for your Get Home Bag should be a good wilderness knife as well as a good fighter. Unless you don't have far to travel in a Get Home/SHTF scenario, then a good fighting knife will suffice. Yes, you can fight with any knife; our American ancestors from the 1700's carried knives that were basically butcher knives. Jeff White Knives recreates these types of knives and they're inexpensive and very good quality.

There are a few different blade types but the most common types found in Fighting knives and Survival Knives are Clip Point and Drop Point. My pocket knife has what's called a spear point which resembles a double edge but the top edge only comes down about half way from the point. It's also a false edge because double edge blades are pretty much illegal to carry just about everywhere.

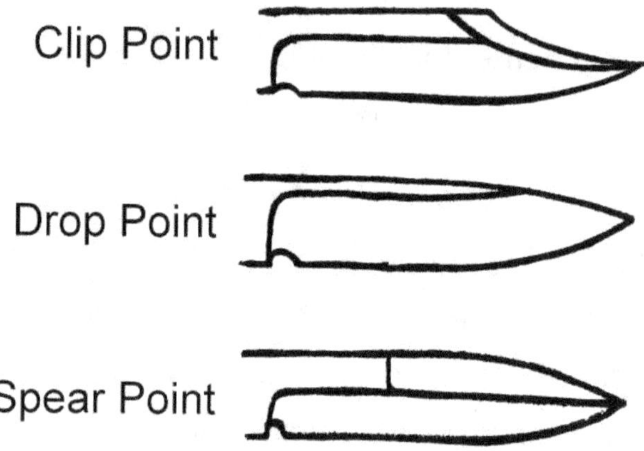

Full tang is the strongest type of knife but there are some knives that have Hidden Tangs that are good. The Pilot's Survival Knife is one that has a robust Stick Tang and can be put through hell. The Kizlyar DV2, used by the Russian Spetsnaz is one of the toughest knives in the world, and has a Hidden Tang as well. The problem with Hidden Tangs is you can't see how robust the tang is; it could be wide and robust or it can be just a thin stick running through the middle of the handle. Stay completely away from Partial Tangs. Most companies mention the Tang construction of the knife in their catalogs. If not and you're interested in purchasing one, give the manufacturer a call and ask them. If they don't tell you then don't buy it.

The Blackjack Halo Model 14 is a good compromise between a Fighting knife and a Bushcraft knife, and has what Blackjack calls a Mortise Tang, which is a full tang but is not the width of the handle. You can only see the Tang from the top of the knife; the handle has a mortise cut and slips on from underneath the Tang.

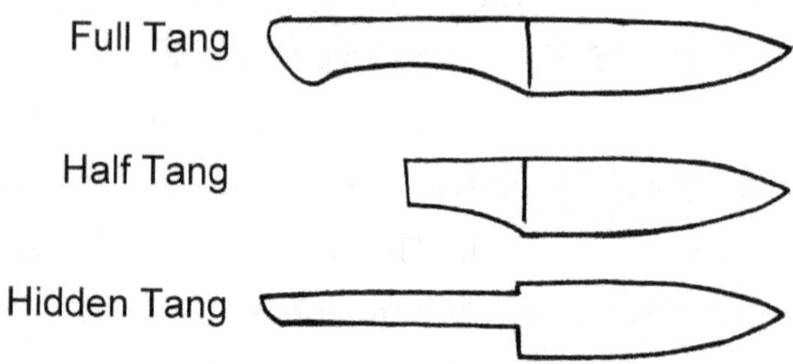

I always have a survival type knife in my EDC so I keep a fighter in my GHB. I chose a SOG Agency because it's very good quality, razor sharp and not all that expensive. I refuse to leave one of my Blackjack Knives in the GHB in my car in case it gets stolen. It won't hurt as much losing the SOG as much as it will if I lost one of my Blackjacks.

Always remember that a knife is a tool and was meant to be used. A fighting knife of course won't be used as much as a Survival knife, but it still should be used for certain tasks, cleaned, and sharpened when it gets dull. If you don't get a feel for your knife now and the basic maintenance you have to do to keep it functional, you're not going to suddenly be enlightened with this information when the SHTF.

I laugh when someone says *"Your knife is all beat up, it lost its value!"* Its *value*? Maybe its monetary value, but I never planned on selling it anyway; I didn't buy it as an investment. I bought it as a tool, and it still holds its value as a knife and a tool, even more so now that I know how it handles, its strengths and its weaknesses, and how to put an edge on it, which reminds me now that I have to sharpen my pocket knife. A friend of someone I once worked with a while back got mad at me for testing the edge of a huge knife he carried on his belt with a sheet of paper. *"Don't cut paper with my knife, you'll ruin the edge!"* he cried, like a little girl. I told him if cutting a sheet of paper will ruin the edge of his blade then it must be a piece of shit. He never used his knife, for anything, ever; it was just for show (and a poor show at that), like wearing a piece of jewelry. Don't be like this guy.

Figure 22- SOG Agency Fighting Knife

First Aid Kit

Even though I saved the First Aid Kit for last it is very important to have in your GHB. What your first aid kit contains depends on your anticipated journey home. The farther you must travel the more items you may wish to pack.

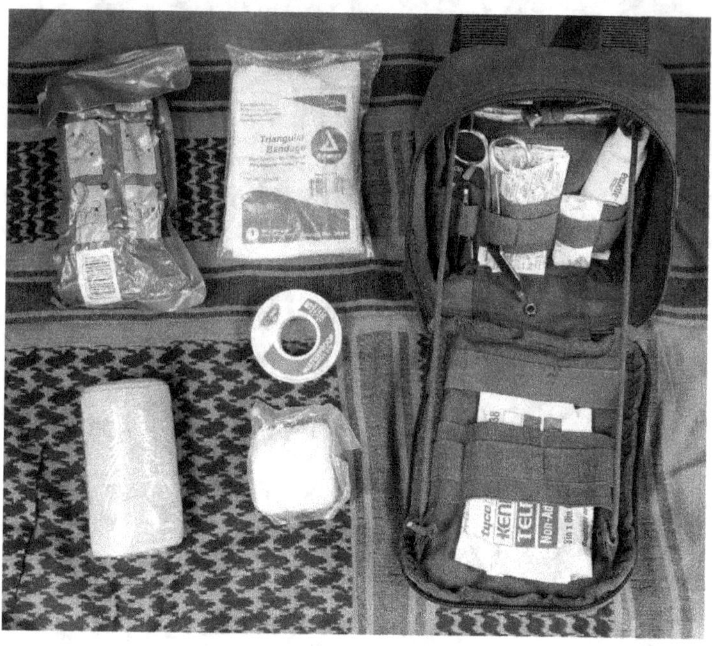

Figure 23- My first aid kit contains an Israeli Bandage, Triangle Bandage, Ace Bandage, Gauze wrap, Medical tape, Scissors, Ointment, Scissors, and various sized bandages.

I attach my first aid kit to the outside of my backpack in a way that I can remove it fast. My pack has MOLLE webbing and rather than weave the MOLLE straps back and forth like you're supposed to, I just slip them through the Webbing on the pack. To remove it all I have to do is unsnap the straps and pull it off. You can purchase hook and loop MOLLE fasteners, and another type of quick release device. But this way is simple, it works, and it doesn't cost anything extra. *Does it bounce around a bit?* Yes, it does, but I don't care.

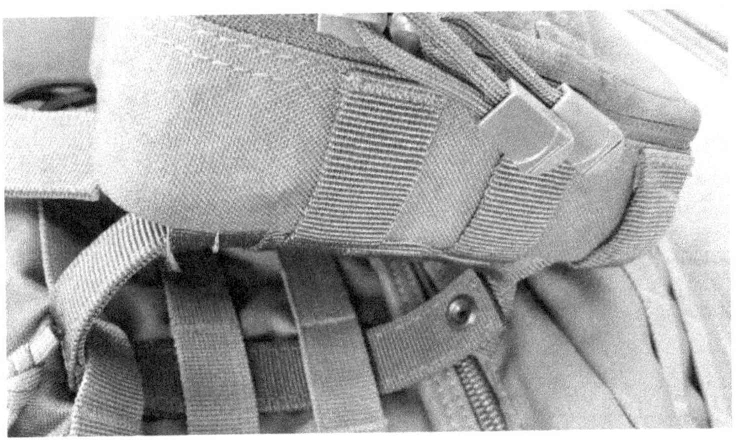

Figure 24- MOLLE straps laced through for quick release.

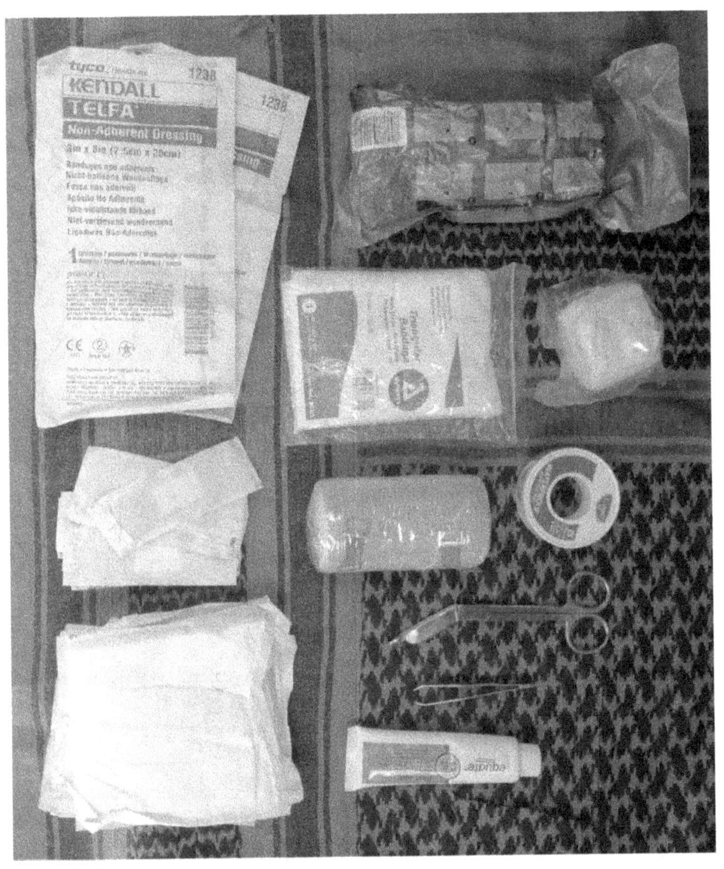

The contents of my First Aid Kit: First row; Two Nonstick Telfa Bandages, band aids, 4x4 gauze bandages, Second row; Israeli Bandage, triangular bandage, Ace bandage, medical scissors, tweezers, antibiotic ointment, roll of gauze, medical tape.

Everything is pretty much self-explanatory and found in all first aid kits in every home, however the Israeli Bandage and the Triangle Bandage might need an explanation.

Israeli Bandage: The Israeli bandage was invented by Bernard Bar-Natan in 1991. It was an idea he worked on and developed since 1984.

The Israeli bandage is an elasticized non-adhesive bandage, 4, 6, or 8 inches wide, with a built-in pressure bar that allows the user to create pressure on the wound. Israeli bandages can be applied with only one hand and are successfully used to stop bleeding and they can also be used as a tourniquet.

Triangular Bandage: A triangular bandage is just a large triangle shaped cotton fabric, but has many first aid applications; it can be used as a sling, or folded as a thick rectangle of cloth and placed over a large wound functioning like a trauma pad, absorbing blood and helping to stop bleeding. It can also be used like an Ace bandage to wrap around sprains. Always keep at least one in your first aid kit.

Figure 25- Moleskin bandages

Moleskin: Moleskin is a fuzzy adhesive bandage that is placed over parts of the foot to prevent blisters. It is made of flexible material that conforms to all the contours of your foot and can be cut to fit any specific area.

Navigation

When I say *Navigation* I don't necessarily mean *finding* your way home, I mean *making* your way home. If you're at work or running errands when the SHTF, I think you'll pretty much know how to get yourself home. The distance you'll be walking home, the terrain, and the weather you'll encounter will all have an effect on the amount of time it takes you to get there.

When deciding what you need in your GHB you have to consider if you'll be walking home in the city, the suburbs, or the wilderness. You might be exposed to two of these environments or possibly even all three! As long as you have fire capability and the means to build a good, temporary shelter relevant to the climate, your GHB could theoretically sustain you weeks, or even months. It's just a matter of having, or the ability to procure, enough food and water. If the distance you anticipate will be more than a three hour walk home you should pack your GHB with items to sustain you overnight. Actually any GHB that is going to be stored in your car should be packed for an overnighter because you never know when or where you'll be when the SHTF.

Three common sense things to know in Navigation are; 1- where you are, 2- where you're going, and 3- how to get there. You should keep the direction of your route open just in case you have to use an alternate route. Consider back roads, logging roads, and maintenance roads if you feel like you have to stay off main roads. Power Lines and State Parks will work if you have to avoid roads altogether, as you mostly should. If your route has any water ways you might be able to commandeer a canoe or a rowboat. It pays to have a good map even if you know the area like the back of your hand, and a compass will keep you from getting disoriented, especially if you have to travel through Power Lines or large State Parks where there are no streets for reference. If you know your area well you'll know which routes to avoid, such as a bad neighborhood or impassable terrain. Google Maps is a great tool because you're actually viewing aerial photographs, and you can print them out. Now is the time to study your area in Google Earth or Google Maps.

Chances are your pack will weigh between 30 and 40 pounds, it can even weigh up to and over 50 pounds if you're packed for a long way from home and have extra supplies to travel over rough terrain. My GHB weighs 30 pounds with my canteens empty and without food. I carry two 1-quart plastic military canteens, filled with water this will add an additional four pounds. (One quart of water weighs approximately two pounds.) My walk home from work is about 10 miles, which is a twenty minute car ride with traffic. Considering the average person walks three miles an hour it would take me a little over three hours to walk that distance, that is if I don't stop to rest, and walk the consistent pace of three miles per hour. Now add humping a 30 plus pound pack to this "three-hour" walk and it can very easily double! Walking with this pack in the summer heat will take a lot longer than walking with it in cool air during the spring or fall. If I get hurt along the way or run into trouble it could take even longer. If you're over a three hour walk from home you should be prepared to hole up for the night; always plan for the worst that can happen.

Map and Compass

Maps have a key that says which way north is, when using a map lay the map on a flat surface, and using your compass rotate the map so it is pointing north, now when you reference the map it will be oriented with the lay of the land. Magnetic north varies a few degrees with true north, and there are deviations within the compass itself, but this is insignificant to the basic navigation you'll be using. The better quality the compass is, the less deviation there will be within the compass. Magnetic north and true north can vary as much as 16 degrees and more depending on where you are. A deviation of 1 degree will be off by one mile for every 60 miles out.

If you print out your maps yourself they might not have the North-South reference on them, but the left and right edges of the map run north and south, and the top and bottom edges run east and west.

Even if you have a road map it might be a good idea to print out a few aerial maps of the routes you'll be traveling through. It's priceless to actually see an aerial photo of a potential bridge, river, or unfamiliar neighborhoods you'll have to cross over or through.

Terrain

City and Suburban

I remember seeing on TV and seeing pictures in the Newspapers of people walking home over the bridges in New York City after the 9/11 attacks on the World Trade Center. If you're in the city or suburbs when the SHTF you'll be amongst a lot of people just trying to make it home. Blend in with a crowd that's going the same way you are, and act naïve, the less people think you know the better. If someone starts asking too many questions about your pack be very vague and fall back a little.

The first day or two after a SHTF scenario most people will be trying to make it home just like you. But on the other hand, some people will be out to hurt other people. During a four hour blackout people start to riot and loot stores; you should know which areas in the city to avoid and stick with the large mass of people until you're away from the city and in an area where you can roll with a smaller group or maybe even go it alone.

A good tool to have in an urban environment is a Sillcock, also called a 4-Way Water Key, or just a Water Key for short (see figure 27). A water key looks like a very small tire iron and works the exact same way. It has four different size square holes in each arm that fit just about every commercial water spout there is. Commercial buildings, schools, and apartment buildings have handle-less water spigots so nobody can just walk up and turn the water on. Maintenance workers carry a water key with them to use the outside water spigots.

Wire cutters (see figure 28) are also an important tool to have in an urban setting. There are so many chain link fences around that you might have to get past one or two, and if you have wire cutters you can go through them instead of going over.

A small tarp would be good to carry in an urban environment. I wouldn't worry about carrying a larger tarp unless your journey home brings you through a rural or wilderness setting. I have a smaller tarp that's sold as an Emergency Blanket. It's really a light duty tarp with grommet holes at each corner, silver Mylar on one side to reflect body heat, and a green color on the other side. They come in various colors, but I chose green for its camouflage capability.

Figure 26- Mylar tarp/emergency blanket

Figure 27: Sillcock or Water Key

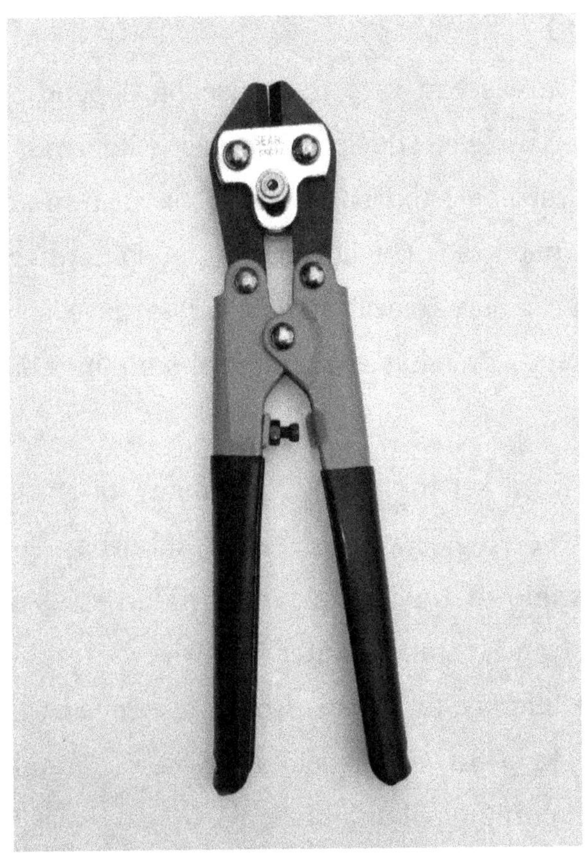

Figure 28: Wire Cutters

Rural

Rural areas can vary in landscape depending on where you live. They can be a vast wilderness with patches of a suburban setting, or vast suburban with patches of wilderness, or somewhere in between. Some rural areas tend to have a lot of farmland, or what's left of farmland in America today.

In a rural setting you'll need many of the same items you'll need in an urban/suburban setting and some of the items for a wilderness setting. This would include a water key, wire cutters, and a small blanket tarp. You would also need a large 8x10 tarp to construct a shelter. A military Entrenching Tool might come in handy as well. You'll have to think about your walk home and determine if a shovel is worth bringing along. A good shovel serves a dual purpose as they can also be used as weapons, especially the Spetznaz shovel with its sturdy handle and sharpened edges on the shovel face.

Figure 29- Spetznaz Shovel

A folding saw is good for cutting firewood and cutting branches to build a shelter. They're lightweight and take up hardly any space, you can lay one flat at the bottom of your pack and you won't even know it's there.

Some rural areas are also known to have bears. If you live in or have to travel through an area with bears you might consider carrying a .500 Magnum handgun. These guns were made for defense from bears; Sport fishermen in Alaska always have them strapped to their hip while they're fishing along the rivers and lakes. Anything smaller might just anger the bear. Some other animals to watch out for depending on where you live are wolves, feral dogs, moose, mountain lions, poisonous snakes and insects. If you live in areas that have these animals you should already have a good idea of how to avoid or deal with them.

The Wilderness

A wilderness setting could be anything from a state park, a wilderness preserve, a mountain range, or just any place that has many square miles of unsettled land. In addition to the wild animals mentioned earlier, you might also encounter natural obstacles like rivers, lakes, or mountains. Even very hilly areas, while not being as challenging as a mountain, will make your trip longer and tire you out faster.

If your walk home will bring you through a wilderness setting longer than one day and night you might want to consider bringing a small forest axe or hatchet. It might be overkill, and it might not be, that's for you to decide if the added weight and space of a small axe is worth adding to your kit. An axe is also dual purpose as it makes a great weapon.

A compass and maps are definitely needed in the wilderness, as there are no familiar streets to orientate yourself.

Small traps and/or snare wire might be good for trapping animals for food. Even a small fishing kit could come in handy. I was once asked by someone if I thought a gill net would be good to have when traversing the wilderness. I personally don't think so as you're not setting up camp for period of time, you're on the move and only stopping to rest or sleep for the night. But again, that choice is up to the individual.

If you have to cross a mountain region you might want to include basic climbing gear. I don't mean all out mountain climbing gear, I mean just the basics. And make sure you get training on how to use any specialized equipment you bring.

Seasons and Weather

Rain

Walking in the rain can definitely slow you down. Not only can it be an inconvenience, it can be life threatening as well. You should try to shelter up in a rain storm, but if you have to travel, keep yourself as dry as possible. You should have a rain suit or a poncho in your GHB, and a change of clothes stored in plastic bags. When traveling in the rain and you have to shelter up for the night, change into your dry clothes to sleep in. Hang your wet clothes up to dry and in the morning change back into your travel clothes whether they're dry or not. The reason being is to keep your change of clothes dry for sleeping. If you wear your sleeping clothes and they too get wet, you'll have nothing dry to sleep in. Sleeping in wet clothes is a good way to get sick and even come down with hypothermia.

In the fall and winter months avoid walking in the rain altogether. Being in wet clothes in colder weather can bring on hypothermia really fast. Hypothermia is when your body temperature goes below 95° F. You can also get hypothermia on chilly summer nights from being in wet clothes. A dry change of clothes is very important in a survival situation.

Cold Weather; Fall and Winter

Make sure you have the proper clothes to wear in the winter. If you're like me in the winter you jump in the car with a t-shirt on and crank up the heat! I do this a lot but I keep a coat, gloves and spare blanket in my car during the winter months. A warm hat would be a good idea to have as well. I have one if those ugly hunting caps with the built in ear covers and it's great! You won't win a beauty contest wearing one but you will be warm. Much of your body temperature is lost through the top of your head. Wearing a hat makes a big difference.

Like I said previously, you should avoid rain altogether in the winter time. Get a shelter built or find someplace to keep dry until the rain stops. Walking while it's snowing a little isn't so bad because it doesn't penetrate your clothing like rain does, but it does do a number on your legs of your pants though, and if your boots aren't waterproof your feet will freeze. I know I said walking while it's snowing is okay, but do not walk during blizzard conditions! If you anticipate a walk home in the snow you might want to consider getting snowshoes.

Snowblind

Snowblindsness is caused when your cornea gets sunburned. This is caused by the reflection of UV light off the snow. When walking in the snow you have to protect your eyes from becoming snowblind. Snowblindness is temporary, but it can last anywhere from 24 to 48 hours, but not being able to see for this amount of time when the SHTF can be deadly, especially if you're alone or have children with you that are depending on you. Sunglasses are important to have if you'll be walking in the snow, even more important than in the summer. If you don't have sunglasses you can cover your eyes with a bandana, cloth, or cardboard with small slits cut into them so you can see through.

Dehydration

Believe it or not you actually lose fluid in the dry air during the winter just as much as in the warm, humid summer months. You have to drink small amounts of water often to keep your fluids at a safe level.

Hypothermia

Normal body temperature is 98.6°F, hypothermia is when your body is exposed to cold temperatures and goes below 95°F. At this point your body loses heat faster than it can produce it, you have to use outside means to bring your body temperature back to normal.

Symptoms of hypothermia include shivering, slurred speech, lack of coordination, low energy, confusion and even loss of consciousness. A person with hypothermia usually isn't even aware they have it as symptoms worsen at a slow pace. If you're with someone in a cold weather SHTF scenario make sure you keep your eyes on each other and know to look for these symptoms. The best bet, especially if you're alone, is if you start to shiver uncontrollably, you should seek a warm, dry shelter immediately.

An Esbit stove with a lot of extra fuel tabs will really help in the winter so you can heat drinking water to keep your core temperature up. Esbit stoves heat up fast and you don't have to worry about building a wood fire to prepare a warm drink.

First Aid for Hypothermia

Immediately upon excessive shivering move to a warm, dry shelter. Remove any wet clothing and cover with dry clothes and a blanket if available. Make sure you are insulated from the cold ground. Ingest warm liquids as soon as possible.

Frostbite

Frostbite is caused when the skin freezes. It usually occurs to your fingers, toes, nose and face.

Any exposed skin in cold, windy weather is vulnerable to frostbite.

The symptoms of frostbite include cold skin and numbness, and discoloration of the skin. Frostbite happens in stages which include; 1-Frostnip; very cold skin that pales or turns red. 2-Superficial Frostbite; ice crystals begin to form on the skin. 3-Severe Frostbite; all layers of the skin are effected. Numbness, pain, and discomfort occur. 24 to 48 hours after warming the affected area will turn black and hard, at this point the skin tissue is dead. Frostbite can occur along with Hypothermia, but can also happen on its own. The risk of frostbite is greater when temperatures reach 5°F and below. Treatment for frostbite is the same as for hypothermia. The best treatment is preventive treatment. Dress for the environment and get yourself warmed up at the first sign of shivering. Rewarm areas susceptible to frostbite gently and slowly. If you must return back into the cold make sure to wrap any suspected frostbitten areas extra good as you don't want the area to refreeze.

Warm Weather; Spring and Summer

Heat can kill you just as cold can. When temperatures reach over 78° you can suffer from heat related illnesses. Especially if the humidity is over 60% you can suffer from Heat Exhaustion, or worse, Heat Stroke. When the humidity is high it slows down the evaporation of your sweat. When sweat evaporates it causes a cooling effect simply called evaporative cooling. Evaporative cooling is most effective when the humidity is 30% or less. As humidity increases the evaporative cooling affect declines; at around 60% humidity is when the lack of evaporative cooling effect can be felt. This is why you feel disgusting when the weather humid.

Dehydration can kill, you always want to watch for dehydration; dark-colored urine is a telltale sign of dehydration. It is easier to prevent dehydration than it is to treat it, drink small anounts of water often and you won't have to worry about inspecting your piss.

Heat Exhaustion

Heat Exhaustion is a heat related illness whose symptoms include confusion, fatigue, fainting, headache, pale skin, profuse sweating, and a rapid heartbeat. Nausea, vomiting, and dizziness can also occur. If you feel any of these ailments you need to rest and rehydrate. If not taken seriously, Heat Exhaustion can lead to Heat Stroke, and without medical attention Heat Stroke will kill you.

Everyone tolerates the heat differently, especially children and the elderly. Don't push anyone or let anyone push you to continue if you or they are complaining about heat exhaustion symptoms. Everyone needs to rest when one person shows the first signs of heat exhaustion.

Avoid traveling on asphalt roads and concrete if you can. Walk in the grass along the side of the road and as far from the road as you can. Asphalt and concrete roadways retain heat and raise the heat index. Even at night the heat is released slowly and will increase the temperature. This can be used to your advantage in colder weather as the roads will be warmer.

First Aid for Heat Exhaustion

If you experience any of the symptoms of heat exhaustion you must get away from the heat and rest. In a SHTF scenario an air conditioned room might be a little hard to find. Get yourself in the shade and remove any tight fitting clothing. Drink plenty of water and use your chilly pad to cool yourself down. After recovering from heat exhaustion you will be more susceptible to warm temperatures for up to a week. You might want to consider resting in the day and traveling at night when the air is cooler, and rest often. Remember to avoid walking directly over the roads as they will still be warmer even at night.

Heat Stroke

Heat Stroke is when your core temperature is greater than 105 °. Heat Stroke is a serious medical emergency, and to avoid it you need to rest and rehydrate at the first sign of fatigue. A personal thermometer would be a good item to carry in your first aid kit, and a small outdoor thermometer is good to throw in your pack. If you are suffering from heat exhaustion and are stubborn about resting and cooling down you will come down with Heat Stroke. A good telltale sign of heat stroke is when you pass out; but you don't want this to happen. Rest and rehydrate at the first sign of heat exhaustion.

First Aid for Heat Stroke

The best treatment for heat stroke is avoiding it. When you feel the symptoms of heat exhaustion coming on you should rest and drink plenty of water. The treatment for heat stroke is the same as heat exhaustion except your chances for survival are severely diminished.

Hypothermia in the summer

Believe it or not you can get hypothermia in the summer. If the night is cool, wet, and windy these are the ingredients for Hypothermia. You need to keep warm and dry. See the Hypothermia section in the Cold Weather section.

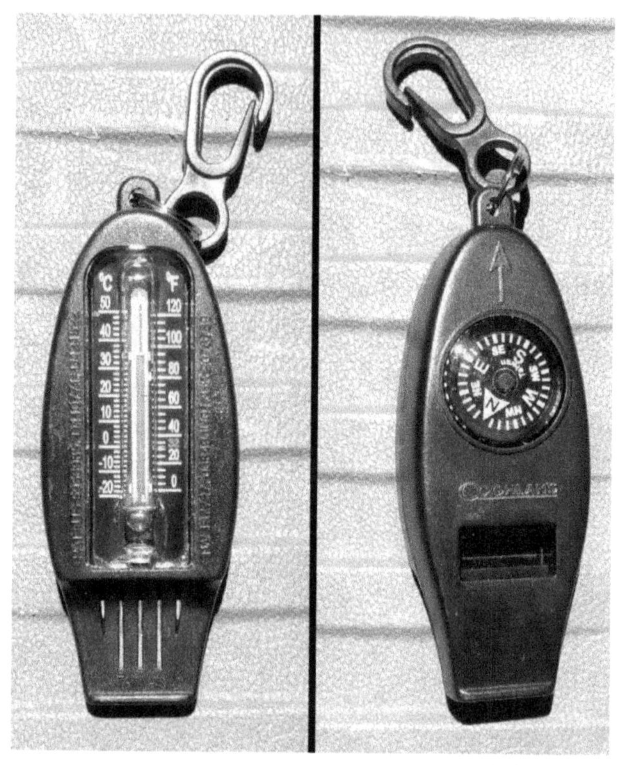

Figure 30- A whistle with thermometer and compass.

Supplemental GHB

A supplemental GHB is a pack stored in your car that someone else can use in conjunction with the main GHB. It just carries a mess kit, a water container, a metal cup, a poncho, and hygiene items to mention a few.

I have three daughters that might be with me in the car. I have three of each of the above items packed inside a small backpack, plus an extra water filter kit, a flashlight, two inexpensive knives and another first aid kit. I also packed two drawstring backpack bags in there as well. If the time arises I can divvy the stuff up so each kid carries their own stuff, with the extra single items staying in the small backpack, so one of the kids will have to carry a little extra. These are all items that I don't mind leaving behind if I'm alone when the SHTF, or I can pass the items along to others to help them get safely home.

In the winter I put three extra coats in the back of the car, along with three pairs of gloves and winter hats. You can throw older coats that the kids don't wear anymore, if they still fit! With hand-me-downs you'll always have one that fits your younger children. Another inexpensive option is to go to a Thrift Store and buy used coats to keep in the car for emergencies.

If you have an infant you would want to pack extra diapers, water and powdered baby formula, or powdered milk if the baby is older. For transporting an infant or younger child a stroller with those "off road" wheels would be great to have. There is also a baby carrier called a Ring Sling that can be worn in many different comfortable positions by the parent.

Kids that are too old for a stroller and walk along with an adult will tire out faster than adults and when they crash, they crash hard! A folding wagon will come in handy for kids to rest while you drag them along behind you. Even an infant can sleep in side a wagon if you make it comfortable for them. You would have to rig a cover overhead on the wagon to keep out the sun and rain. A light colored umbrella would work well or a jacket or piece of cloth, just like a covered wagon. Carrying an older kid is not practical when you're wearing a thirty pound back pack. Even if you threw the kid on your shoulders it would be an extra fifty or so pounds, now you're humping an extra eighty pounds or so, some people can do it, but most of us can't. Even if you can do it, overexerting yourself isn't helpful to you or the child that is depending on you.

Kids any age would also need some kind of quiet toy like a stuffed animal. I say quiet because a toy that makes noise could compromise your position in certain situations.

Figure 31- Some of my youngest daughter's toys. Even the simplest toy can keep a child occupied for hours. Just make sure the cap guns don't have caps in them.

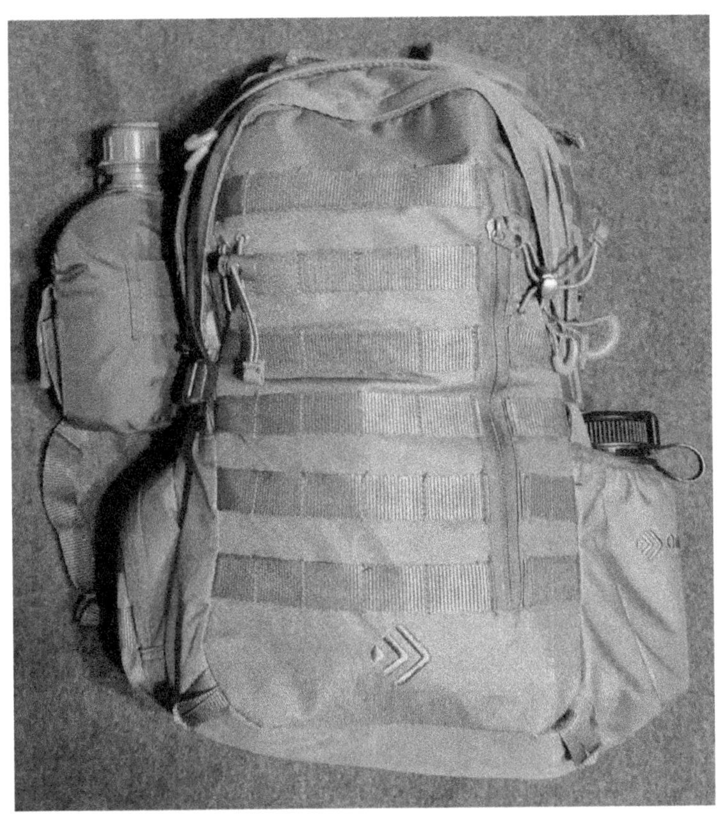

This small bag holds all the supplemental gear for my three children. You can see the canteen and one of the water bottles on the outside of the pack. The canteen has a steel canteen cup, and there are two steel cups inside the bag with the third water bottle. If the SHTF and I'm alone I will grab the extra water filter, the canteen and canteen cup, and leave the rest of the things behind where someone can find them, or pass them off to others.

The picture above shows the supplemental water kit, and two inexpensive but good quality knives for my two older children.

This picture shows one of the water bottles and one of the steel cups from inside the supplemental GHB.

Special Considerations for Kids

Cold Weather

Make sure children are dressed for the weather; they need to dress warmer than adults. Children lose heat faster than adults, once a child starts shivering get to a warm shelter immediately!

Hot Weather

Children up to age four are more susceptible to heat than adults. Make sure children keep cool in hot weather. As I mentioned earlier, walk along the side of the road in the grass if possible, not over the hot pavement. Rest and rehydrate often. Ask children often if they're thirsty and let them know to tell you right away if they feel thirsty or too hot.

Scrounged items

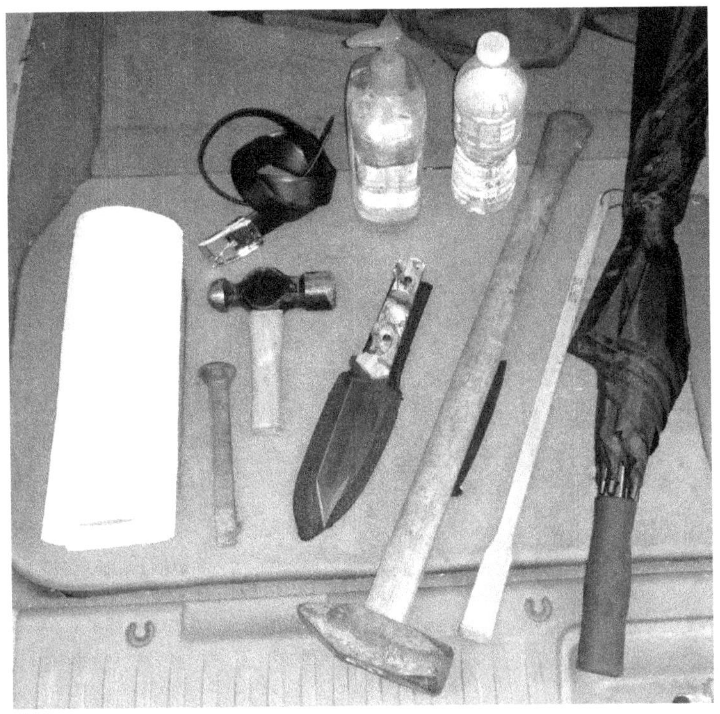

In the photo above are items I scrounged from my car. I found a roll of paper towels, a rusty rail road spike, a sledge hammer, a ballpeen hammer, a crappy knife, a belt, hand sanitizer, an umbrella, a back scratcher, and a half empty water bottle. This is stuff I grabbed in less than five minutes. I also have in the car a Picnic Ground Cover, maps, empty soda cans, fast food napkins, and a small tool bag with repair tools, among other things; my car is a mess! Are all of these things practical? Maybe, maybe not, but it's just an example of useful items you might be able to scrounge up in an emergency.

The water bottle is another water container, you can never have too many. The hand sanitizer will of course keep your hands sanitary. The knife, hammers and spike can all be used as weapons. The paper towels are for when nature calls or can be used to help start fires. The backscratcher is indispensable, if you've ever used one you'll agree! The umbrella of course will keep you dry in the rain. I know it's hard to look cool while using an umbrella, buts it's even harder to look dry when not using one! If I'm using a wagon to transport my stuff I can throw all of these items in to hand out to people I meet along the way that might be in need. If I pick up a travel partner that I trust I might pass him the knife and sledge hammer. Of course if I don't have a wagon or a shopping cart I would leave this crap behind. Almost everything you find has some kind of use, you have to use your imagination and weigh out whether or not it's worth the extra weight to bring with you. Even along your route home you could check out abandoned cars and trucks to see if there's anything inside that you can use.

Items in my GHB

Now it's time to check out what's currently in my GHB. My pack is constantly changing and evolving so the items I currently have might not match everything I said throughout this book. But that's the nature of the beast; your bag should change and evolve as well. You might learn a new skill and add a corresponding item 'to your pack, or you might look through your bag and ask yourself what in the hell made you decide to put that thing in there to begin with! That's part of process, you should check your bag every three months or so anyway to make sure everything is in good working order, your batteries are still good, your son or daughter didn't "borrow" something, or whatever the case may be.

I currently use a Voodoo Tactical Reaper Large MOLLE Military Patrol Pack. The Reaper is a pretty good pack for its price. It's a 2500 cubic inch main compartment and has a bottom section that expands to hold another 850 cubic inches.

From the front view of the Voodoo Reaper you can see two military 2-quart canteens, my first aid kit, a shemagh, in the plastic bag you see behind the shemagh is my cooling towel.

These are the items that came out of the front pocket that you see below the shemagh. Starting top left and going clockwise is a water tight case that holds fire starting material, matches, a lighter, and a P-51 can opener, a pair of binos; 7-15 x 25, a folding saw, wire cutters. Work gloves, a hygiene kit; mouthwash, deodorant, toothbrush and tooth paste, two washcloths. I also have my Esbit stove, a larger bottle of mouthwash and bug repellant in the pocket.

This is the expandable bottom section. I keep it zipped up because I don't have much stuff inside. It holds my poncho, rain pants, maps secured in a plastic bag, and a small plastic cutting board.

This is the main compartment. Inside you can see my mess tin pie plate, tin cup with water filter, toilet paper, above the pie tin, near the top of the bag is a plastic case that holds 50 rounds of ammo, under the ammo and behind the pie tin is my compact sleeping bag, to the right of the ammo box are a pair of sunglasses and a blue rain cover for the pack. Behind everything is a rolled up tarp and my emergency blanket/tarp, a change of clothes, contractor bags, a bath towel, and tent spikes. Also tucked inside is my SOG Agency Fighting Knife.

The picture above is the contents of the mesh pocket. Starting from the left and going down each row is; blanket pins, a pack of razor blades, lifeboat matches in a waterproof case, a lighter, an all in one whistle/thermometer/compass, water purification tablets, a figure 9 device, metal camping utensils, paracord, light sticks, a bandana, and a mylar emergency blanket. In the other mesh pocket is a spare pair of eye glasses, and a lighter inside a plastic storage container.

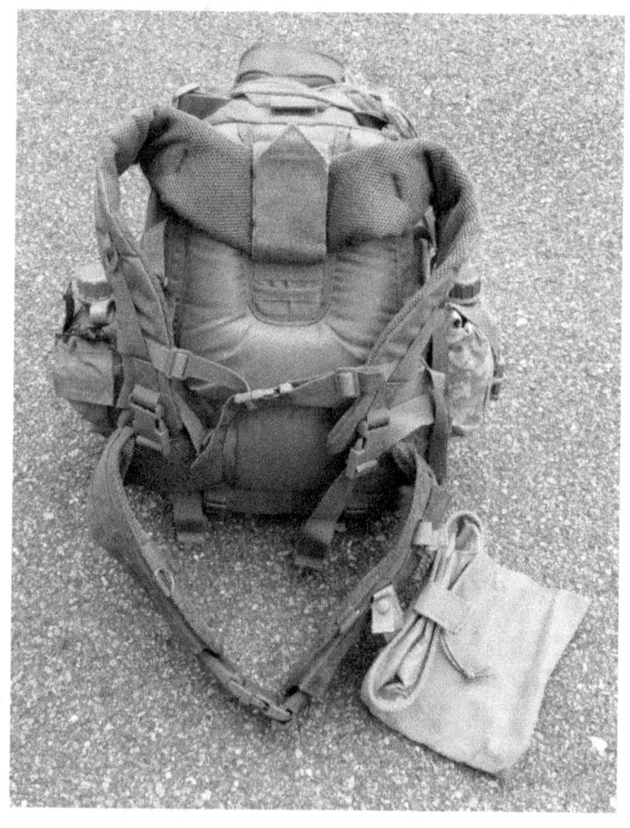

Figure 32- The back of my GHB

The above picture (fig. 24) is the back of the pack. I didn't like the waist belt that came with the Reaper pack so I changed it out with a regular Battle Belt. Attached to the battle belt is a Dump Pouch. A dump pouch is good to have if you find items along the way you can just drop them in the pouch. Or you can keep a water bottle and snacks inside to eat and drink on the move.

Further Reading

In no particular order.

-*The Gift of Fear* - Gavin de Becker

-*The Backpacker's Field Manual*- Rick Curtis

-*Six Ways In And Twelve Ways Out*- George W. Jasper, U.S. RSOG

-*The Things They Carried*- Tim O'Brien

-*Light's Out*- Ted Kopple

-*The Modern Survival Manual: Surviving the Economic Collapse*- Fernando "Ferfal" Aguirre

-*Survivalist Family Prepared Americans for a Strong America*- Joseph Fox

-*Going Home*- A. American

-*The Reluctant Partisan, Volume One: The Guerrilla*- John Mosby

- *We Die Alone*- David Howarth

-*The Book of Camping & Woodcraft*- Horace Kephart

-Woodcraft and Camping- Nessmuk

-EMP Attacks and Solar Storms- Arthur T. Bradley, Ph.D.

-Boston's Gun Bible- by Boston T. Party.

-Stalking The Wild Asparagus- Euell Gibbons

-When All Hell Breaks Loose- Cody Lundin

www.ingramcontent.com/pod-product-compliance
Lightning Source LLC
Chambersburg PA
CBHW050811260726
48660CB00004B/1364